Towards Successful Learning

Introducing a model for supporting and guiding
successful learning and teaching in schools

Diana Pardoe

Published by Network Educational Press
PO Box 635
Stafford
ST16 1BF
www.networkpress.co.uk

First published 2005
© Diana Pardoe 2005

ISBN-13:   978 1 85539 199 4
ISBN-10:   1 85539 199 6

Managing editor: Janice Baiton
Design, typesetting and cover: Neil Hawkins – Network Educational Press Ltd

Printed in Great Britain by Ashford Colour Press Ltd, Gosport, Hants.

Contents

Foreword

I think the only thing we can guarantee on our journey through life is that we will sometimes get stuck, sometimes get fed up and sometimes get lost.

If our education system is to be of worth, it must teach our young learners what to do when each or all of these happen in their lives.

What makes us successful in life is not necessarily what we know, but our capacity to respond positively when we do get stuck, or fed up or lost on our learning journey. The attitudes we develop when we are young will help or hinder us as we search for the 'treasures' that learning offers. The attitudes we model as adults impact on young learners with some force, positively or negatively. Our responsibility, as older learners, is to make sure we model what we want young learners to do. I often ask teachers these questions:

➤ When you stand up in front of your class do you model how to teach or do you model how to learn?

➤ How many of your children will be teachers when they grow up?

➤ How many of your children will be learners when they grow up?

Many teachers can share what they do to demonstrate good teaching but too many teachers find it a struggle to share what they do to demonstrate good learning. This book explores the ideas of good learning and emphasizes the importance of co-responsibility in the learning process.

I would like all adults, not just teachers, to model a love of learning, to inspire children to want to find out more, to demonstrate what a motivated adult looks like when they are learning and to enable our young learners to remove the barriers they come across on their journey.

Let's make sure we practise what we preach.

Tom Robson
Advisory Team Leader (Learning, Assessment and Science)
Wiltshire County Council
May 2005

Acknowledgements

I would like to acknowledge my sincere appreciation for all the support, advice and challenge I have received from pupils and staff in the Success@Excellence in Cities Action Zone. I am privileged to work with such talented and committed teaching and support staff, whose contributions to this book have been invaluable.

In particular I would like to thank the following:

Fair Furlong Primary School, Bristol, especially
Peter Overton, headteacher
Angela Craig, teacher
Annabel Davis, teacher
Christine Clark, teacher

Headley Park Primary School, Bristol, especially
Mavis Rayford, headteacher
Andy Nash, deputy headteacher

Highridge Infant School, Bristol, especially
Genny Oliver, acting headteacher
Anne Peart, teacher
Vikki Hallett, teacher

Teyfant Community School, Bristol, especially
Gus Grimshaw, headteacher
Sarah Clifford, deputy headteacher
Vourneen Carter, teacher

Introduction

Education is not filling a bucket, but lighting a fire.

W. B. Yeats

Learning is a journey not a race. This journey takes us to many places – some of them are bright and sunny, some are dark and less comfortable – all, however, teach us something if we are prepared to learn from our varied experiences and help us towards the next destination.

Recent research into learning and the emerging philosophies promote an approach to learning that focuses more on the 'active participant' than on the 'passive recipient'. However, in the twenty-first century we still live with a system that measures the achievements of our young people using a series of narrow, high-stakes assessments that focuses more on the acquisition of knowledge than on the development of young people as learners.

Because of the constant pressure schools are under to perform and raise achievement, and to 'set and get' ever-increasing targets, teachers live with conflict and tension.

Is it more expedient to grab at a 'quick fix' that seems to solve the immediate problems, or follow a route that requires a longer-term investment?

This book explores the relationship between the levels of pupils' engagement and independence in their learning, their intrinsic motivation and experience of success, and the impact in terms of deeper levels of learning, where there has been negotiation and collaboration with learners regarding their tasks.

Surely the major 'stakeholder' in education is the learner? Yet, pupils have often been expected to perform in a vacuum where they are given a set of instructions in order to complete a task without being given the purpose of the task or how it fits into a meaningful context.

We need to ask ourselves some serious questions:

➤ Why are so many young people disaffected?

➤ Why are ever-increasing numbers of young people committing suicide – particularly boys and young men?

➤ Why do so many young people turn to drugs for some sort of solution to their problems?

➤ Why is youth crime at an all-time high?

Could the way in which we educate our children be a contributory factor to any of the above? If the answer is 'yes', surely we have an obligation to do something about it!

It is well documented that learners demonstrate increased self-esteem, greater independence and ultimately higher achievement when they are involved in the development and understanding of their own learning experiences. Pupils can frequently become disengaged, disenchanted and, subsequently, disaffected. Yet, when given greater opportunities for decision making and greater autonomy in their learning, they generally demonstrate greater motivation and perseverance.

The more learners are encouraged to ask questions and to seek solutions, the more they are likely to become intrinsically motivated by the learning process.

This book examines the key principles that underpin successful learning and draws significantly upon the research in assessment for learning of Paul Black and Dylan Wiliam (1998), the Assessment Reform Group (1999, 2002) and the work of Shirley Clarke (2001, 2003).

The Successful Learner Model

The Successful Learner Model is drawn from classroom practice; however, frequent references are made to research and literature that support and underpin the principles of the model. I have been developing the model over the past two years, working with colleagues in action zone schools. The teachers with whom I have worked have played a hugely significant role in the way the model has evolved, and Chapter 5 contains some case studies from these schools where the model has been implemented.

The model is designed to encapsulate and hold together the key elements of what constitutes effective learning. It attempts to identify what learners need in order to be successful and, therefore, what it is that teachers need to do in order to enable successful learning to take place. Underpinning all the elements is a commitment to the development of successful learning.

The Successful Learner Model takes the form of a three-dimensional jigsaw puzzle. The top layer identifies the key principles that underpin successful learning, while the second layer offers a more explicit description of these principles. This will be explained in greater depth in Chapter 3.

The top layer of the learner puzzle is presented on the following page, since it is helpful to see the model at an early stage. It is, however, very important to take time to encourage focused discussion about the nature of learning and the optimum conditions for learning before engaging with the model itself.

The icon shown here appears on those pages in this book that can be found on the accompanying CD-ROM and used as photocopiable resources within the purchasing institution. The disk also contains some blank resource pages so you can add your own text.

To be a successful learner I need to ...

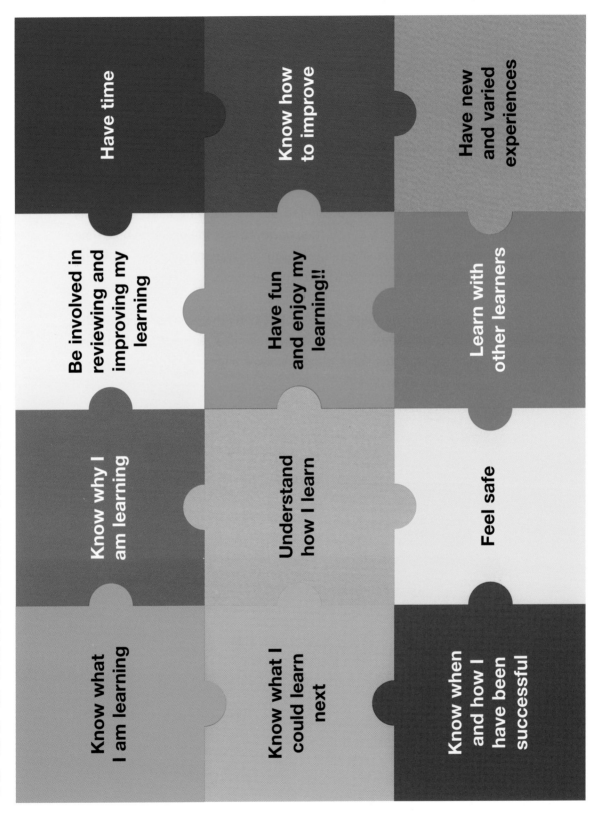

10

Know what
I am learning

Know why I
am learning

Be involved in
reviewing and
improving my
learning

Have time

Know what I
could learn
next

Understand
how I learn

Have fun
and enjoy my
learning!!

Know how
to improve

Know when
and how I
have been
successful

Feel safe

Learn with
other learners

Have new
and varied
experiences

2 Learning about the learners

*Teachers affect eternity; they can
never tell where their influence stops.*

The central tenet of this book is how significant it is for learners to take an active role in their learning and how this relates to their achievement. Many reflective teachers have, for some considerable time, been concerned with the lack of motivation and underachievement in their young learners. In considering why this is the case and what can be done to improve the situation, teachers frequently report that:

➤ the curriculum is overloaded and too prescriptive

➤ children are not involved enough in the learning process since the pressure to cover the objectives and produce evidence leaves too little time for reflection and interaction (see Chapter 4)

➤ success is narrowly defined using grades and numbers.

The Successful Learner Model has evolved from reflective practice and action research in schools and classrooms. Teachers are continually attempting to manage an ever-increasing number of initiatives and strategies. All too often these are perceived as ends in themselves, being mutually exclusive and therefore often managed in isolation from each other; for example, National Curriculum Programmes of Study, National Literacy Strategy, National Numeracy Strategy, QCA Schemes of Work, Assessment for Learning, Excellence and Enjoyment and so on. If we liken these initiatives to plants, then the Successful Learner Model is the soil in which these plants take root and grow.

The principal functions of the Successful Learner Model are to help:

➤ teachers and learners engage together in high-quality learning conversations

➤ learners recognize the complexity of learning

➤ learners engage with learning by exploring different ways of working.

It is crucial that as teachers we aim to increase the self-efficacy as well as the self-esteem of young learners. There are those whose self-esteem may be high, in that they are valued as individuals by families and friends, but whose self-efficacy is low, in that they regard themselves as unsuccessful or poor learners (Clarke, 2003).

If learners are to develop self-efficacy, it is vital that they have a clear understanding of what is expected: specific criteria for recognizing progress and success, supportive and constructive feedback and opportunities to review and revise their learning – all key features of assessment for learning and central to the development of the successful learner. In discussions with children about their learning, many have indicated that they often understand what they are doing but are less sure of what they are actually learning and of how their tasks and activities are relevant.

The Successful Learner Model is an attempt to support and guide learners and practitioners in making sense of learning. When learners (of any age) gain a deeper understanding of what it is that underpins learning and teaching activity, they develop an increased ability to recognize skills, strengths and areas of difficulty, and, importantly, an increased awareness of how to improve.

The classroom climate needs to be embedded with the belief that all pupils can learn and improve.

As professional educators we understand that effective learning involves long-term investment, and yet lack of time is often identified as being the reason why significant ideas do not become embedded in practice. Many teachers recognize what needs to happen in order to improve the quality of *learning* in their classrooms, and yet they feel constrained by timetables and an overloaded curriculum, added to which the pressure to raise attainment is constant and so, understandably, 'quick fixes' are often seized upon as solutions. Just as with any investment, the more we can afford to put in at the beginning, the greater the payout at the end – if we concentrate intensively on developing optimum conditions for and positive attitudes to learning, then progress will ultimately accelerate.

The Learner Profile

Learners need time to talk both informally and formally about their learning and about how they perceive themselves as learners. They also need time to think about their learning, how they feel about learning and what would help them to improve. If as teachers we are to receive honest responses, we must ensure that our classrooms are safe and supportive environments where individuals feel confident in expressing their views and opinions. If this is not the case, we will simply receive responses designed to give the information that the learner thinks that the teachers want!

A comprehensive list of questions used to explore the perceptions and attitudes of learners is provided on page 15, and five of these questions are selected for a Learner Profile on page 16. Some examples from Key Stage 2 pupils are shown on pages 17–18.

Where the response to question 1 is positive, the most common reasons given are that learning is interesting, exciting, fun or useful for the future. Where the response is negative, the most common reasons are boredom, lack of understanding or feeling anxious.

The most frequently observed responses to question 2 are: working with a partner or in a group, getting individual help when needed, clear explanation from the teacher, resources around the room, talking through the task and thinking time. The responses to question 4 largely re-emphasize the importance of these elements identified by the children as being significant in helping them to learn.

In considering what it is that stops learning (question 3), the overwhelming reason given is distraction. This is further elaborated upon as: too much noise, being interrupted or disturbed, the teacher talking too much, (inappropriate) talking to friends. The other most common responses to this question are anxiety, and feeling tired or uncomfortable.

It is clear from the responses to question 5 that many learners think there are methods that they can use themselves to become more successful learners: concentrating more and focusing on the task, asking for help, thinking about where to sit and who to work with, and 'having a go'.

Thus, it appears that many young learners recognize what they need to support them with their learning, and can identify situations and incidents that prevent them from engaging fully. We have a clear responsibility as educators to listen to our learners and to endeavour to meet their learning needs.

It is interesting to observe that teachers and learners frequently identify similar features that they feel would enhance learning experiences, since it is often these same features that are missing in many classrooms. For example:

➤ learners recognize the need for *thinking time*

➤ teachers understand the importance of *reflection time* for consolidating learning

➤ lessons are often full of activity leaving *little or no time* for thinking and reflection.

The Successful Learner Model attempts to bring together the key elements of high-quality learning and teaching in a practical, accessible form that helps to make sense of modern learning theory.

Whatever the model, programme or project, however impressive the resources, it is people who make the difference. Improvements in practice require changes in practice and therefore require practitioners who are optimistic and responsive to change; individuals who are positive, enthusiastic and creative; individuals who are reflective and wish to improve; individuals who Brighouse defines as 'energy creators'. There are the staff who will have a positive effect upon those who are competent and willing; these are the 'energy neutral' individuals. There are also, in any organization, those individuals who have a negative outlook and who are unable or unwilling to change; individuals who may have low self-esteem themselves, whose sense of identity may be weakened. These are the 'energy consumers' (Brighouse and Woods, 1999). Clearly organizations wishing to improve need a critical mass of energy creators and, certainly, individuals who are 'never less than neutral' (Brighouse and Woods, 1999).

Many teachers feel that their sense of identity has been eroded in recent years by the stream of external programmes and strategies that have been imposed in the drive to raise standards. This is of particular significance in urban areas where attainment is generally lower than the national averages (Reed, 2004). Ultimately, this may contribute to the damaging of teacher confidence and the creating of greater dependency on external 'experts'. It may be that some teachers, therefore, feel more secure with a 'tick list' in front of them than being placed in a position where they feel exposed and vulnerable. There may be avoidance of conflict and loss of trust, both of which are crucial to reflecting critically on practice in order to improve (Hargreaves, 2004).

The Successful Learner Model is a professional development tool that provides a starting point for teachers to share their perceptions of learning processes against a set of principles and this can lead to an increase in confidence and a deeper understanding.

Learner Profile Questions

1   Do you enjoy learning? Why?

2   What do you think helps you to learn?

3   What do you think stops you from learning?

4   What can your teacher do to help you to be a successful learner?

5   What can you do yourself to be a successful learner?

6   What do you do when you get 'stuck'?

7   How do you feel when you get 'stuck'?

8   How do you feel when you are asked to work on your own?

9   How do you feel when you are asked to work in a group?

10   How do you feel when you are asked to answer a question on your own?

11   How do you feel when you are asked to answer a question as a team member?

12   How do you feel when you make a mistake/get something wrong?

13   How do you feel when you receive praise from your teacher?

14   How do you feel when you receive praise from your group/team/other people in your class?

15   What is the jigsaw for?

16   Can you tell me about the successful learner jigsaw?

17   How does the successful learner jigsaw help you with your learning?

18   What is your learning target at the moment?

Learner Profile	
for:	
from:	**School**
Do you enjoy learning? Why?	
What do you think helps you to learn?	
What do you think stops you from learning?	
What can your teacher do to help you to be a successful learner?	
What can you do yourself to become a successful learner?	
Date completed:	

Learner Profile

for:
from: Year 5 pupil   School

Do you enjoy learning? Why?	yes I enjoy learning because it helps us when we are older.
What do you think helps you to learn?	working as a team helps me learn Dictionaries and things around the room.
What do you think stops you from learning?	when we are working on our own and someone talking to you I get distracted.
What can your teacher do to help you to be a successful learner?	write in our books what we red in are improving
What can you do yourself to become a successful learner?	by listening at the teacher constantly. Talking to a partner and checking my work with a partner.
Date completed:	12·5·04

Learner Profile

for: Year 5 pupil   School
from:

Do you enjoy learning? Why?	Yes, because sometimes its fun as well.
What do you think helps you to learn?	Books, dictionary, Partner, team, words to help and the teacher explaining it.
What do you think stops you from learning?	getting distracted when I'm right into it. When it's hot. Can't see board. Can't hear teacher.
What can your teacher do to help you to be a successful learner?	Explain well and make sure I understand.
What can you do yourself to become a successful learner?	Try my best. Concentrate well. Listen to the teacher.
Date completed:	12·5·04

Learner Profile   DATE: 12/5/04

School

for:
from: Year 5 pupil

Do you enjoy learning? Why?	& no because we all argue and its boring!
What do you think helps you to learn?	The things around the classroom and working with a partner.
What do you think stops you from learning?	I get distracted and talking and its working on my own.
What can your teacher do to help you to be a successful learner?	Miss Clark can help by giving me ideas.
What can you do yourself to become a successful learner?	I can do try to listen, concentrate and look at the stuff around the room.
Date completed: 12/5/04	

Learner Profile

School

for: Year 5 pupil
from:

Do you enjoy learning? Why?	Yes, because it helps me to get on with other things in my life.
What do you think helps you to learn?	Talking to people who don't just give me the answer, they help me solve the problem with methods.
What do you think stops you from learning?	Distractions, hotness and coldness. Worrying!
What can your teacher do to help you to be a successful learner?	Give us more information and facts before asking us to do a challenge.
What can you do yourself to become a successful learner?	Concentration, try to avoid distractions, try to avoid anything that would stop me learning.
Date completed:	

Learning is a puzzle!

Successful learning occurs when learners have ownership of their learning; when they understand the goals they are aiming for; when crucially they are motivated and have the skills to achieve success.

Assessment Reform Group (1999)

What makes a successful learner?

In order to examine this question it is necessary to establish what is meant by successful. Schools are judged upon their percentages of A* to C grades at GCSE or level 4+ at the end of Key Stage 2. This implies that to do this is to be successful. Is it then being suggested that pupils who do not achieve five A* to C GCSEs are unsuccessful? Are they then without value? The constant pressure upon schools to increase these percentages results in many pupils 'writing themselves off', as they feel marginalized and without value in a system of high-stakes assessment that measures only a narrow field of what they have learned.

So why the Successful Learner Model?

The 'Successful Learner Model' title perhaps needs elaborating. When located in a thesaurus, 'success' is found to have synonyms such as *eminence*, *fame*, *accomplishment*, *achievement*, *mastery*, *attainment*, *victory*, *fortune* and *happiness*. When asked what they understand by 'success', many young learners give responses that focus upon:

➤ levels and grades, such as 'getting a four in my SATS', 'getting a C grade or higher in my GCSEs'

➤ being first, being the best, winning

➤ external rewards – stickers, merits, prizes.

Children need to see being SUCCESSFUL in the wider context of achieving something new for the first time, improving their own personal performance and reaching their own goals. Although this may seem straightforward, there are many needs to be met before conditions are conducive to successful learning experiences.

In exploring motivation and learning, the source of self-worth and the experience of success, the best place to start is in the classroom, talking to children about their lives and their learning, and providing them with the language of learning. Unless as teachers we give time and attention to the self-esteem and motivation of each LEARNER, unless we recognize and value difference and unless we invest time in creating a healthy, safe environment for learning, we are probably wasting our time.

The use of the term MODEL is deliberate. It makes the point that this is not yet another initiative, project or strategy, but an exemplar that identifies and attempts to link and make sense of the key elements of effective learning and teaching in a holistic sense.

When establishing a positive climate for learning with a new class, it is always useful to ask the following three questions:

1 What do you want your teacher to be like?

2 What do you want the classroom to be like? (List/chart the responses to these questions so that everyone can see them.)

3 So what are YOU going to do? (In order to enable your teacher and classroom to be as you wish!)

To foster a real sense of ownership it is crucial that learners, of any age, are given opportunities to identify their own learning needs rather than be told what they are by the teacher.

The Successful Learner Model is first introduced in professional staff development sessions. Teachers then use similar activities with their classes. This requires an important commitment from the teachers in dedicating significant class time to sessions that are not explicitly timetabled or subject focused.

Before the Successful Learner Model is introduced, it is important to engage teachers and/or learners in focused discussions about their learning. A useful activity that generates powerful conversations about learning is given opposite.

Movers and blockers

For this activity learners work in small groups to identify what helps them to learn (movers) and what stops them from learning (blockers).

Question 1

What helps you to learn? (Three minutes to brainstorm ideas and a further three minutes to discuss and then prioritize the top three ideas from the group.)

Question 2

What stops you from learning? (Again, three minutes to brainstorm ideas and a further three minutes to discuss and then prioritize the top three ideas from the group.)

It is very important that those engaged in this activity respond to the questions from their own perspective as learners. For example, when teachers are working together, they need to consider how *they* feel as adult learners, not how they *think* the children in their classes feel about learning.

From the lists created, group members then explore together what *successful learners do* (examples follow).

It is important that the question is phrased 'What does a successful learner do?' so that the responses given include a verb, such as *listens*, *thinks*, *tries hard*, *asks questions* or *reads*. This emphasizes that specific actions are required to become successful in learning.

From the verbs used, specific observable behaviours can then be identified that illustrate the action. For example:

You have said that a successful learner listens.
What does that look like/sound like in our classroom/staffroom/school?

You have said that a successful learner takes care of things.
What does that look like/sound like in our classroom/setting?

You have said a successful learner makes sure he/she understands what to do.
What does that look like/sound like in our classroom/school?

This focus on observable behaviours does not, however, mean a behaviourist approach to learning. The surface behaviours act as a starting point from which learners are facilitated to construct meaningful understanding and greater ownership of their learning.

The responses also provide evidence of the language that learners are using to articulate their thinking about learning, creating opportunities for teachers to build upon and develop learners' language skills and vocabulary. The more effective learners are at communicating their thinking, their understanding and, importantly, their misunderstanding, the more involved they become in their own learning and the more enabled teachers are to differentiate the learning and provide appropriate challenge, guidance or support.

What does a successful learner do?

Some responses to this question made by children working with a partner are provided on pages 23 and 24, and a poster incorporating all the responses of a class of Year 4 and 5 children to the question is shown on page 25.

The class had previously identified what helps them learn and what stops them from learning, had some personal reflection time, and then worked with a partner to respond to the question. The poster is displayed and is then used interactively in the classroom, particularly in review and reflection sessions.

What Does A Successful Learner Do?

- Find out new things.
- Listening.
- Practice.
- Trying your hardest.
- carry on going on and don't give up.

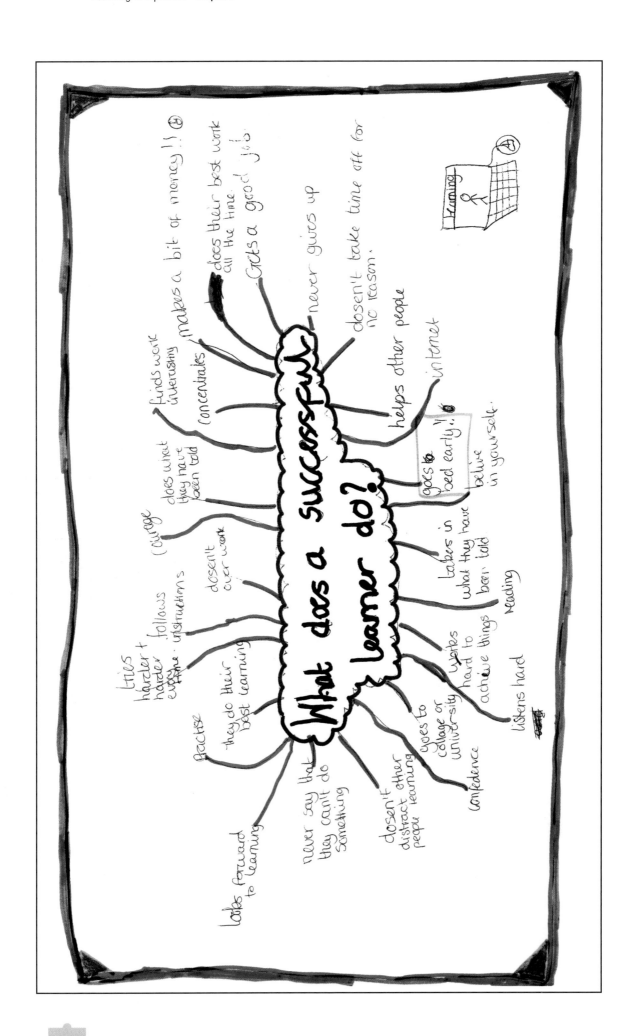

- Believes in herself/himself
- Looks forward to learning

- Listens to the teacher and other people in the class
- Tells the truth

- Never says 'I can't do it'

- Thinks hard
- Keeps healthy
- Goes to bed early!

- Never stops trying
- Concentrates hard

- Doesn't skip school!
- Works with other people
- Focuses on what to do

What does a successful learner do?

- Asks questions
- Joins in
- Uses books

- Listens carefully
- Doesn't distract others

- Has confidence
- Always does his/her best

- Helps other people
- Behaves well
- Takes care of things

- Tries harder every time

- Uses her/his brain
- Brainstorms ideas and thinking

- Makes sure he/she understands what to do

- Talks about work with a friend
- Follows instructions
- Does as asked

- Has the courage to have a go!
- Finds work interesting

Year 4 and Year 5 learners

What is it that learners NEED in order to be successful?

The next step is to explore what needs to be in place to enable successful learning to happen, where successful learning incorporates all the actions identified.

Learners need to know what they are learning and the purposes for that learning and how it 'fits' into a bigger picture that is relevant and meaningful. They need to know what is expected of them and how they can achieve success. They need to be fully involved in the whole learning process, developing the skills they need to identify how they are doing, what they need to do next and, crucially, how to 'close the gap'. Learners need time to reflect, time to ask questions and to seek solutions, and time to talk to and collaborate with peers and adults.

The central aim of the Successful Learner Model is to support and guide teachers in maximizing the involvement of pupils in their own learning, and gradually transferring some responsibility of the learning to the learner. The Ofsted Annual Report states that in unsatisfactory lessons, typically, the expectations are too low, the learning fails to challenge and 'pupils are given insufficient opportunities to engage in purposeful discussion and interaction' (Ofsted, 2004).

Learning is complex and multifaceted, and thus visual representation is not easy. After exploration of a range of ideas and concepts, the final outcome has taken the form of a jigsaw puzzle, where all the pieces have to be in place for learning to be really successful. Just as completing a jigsaw puzzle is an experience very common to both children and adults, so too is the frustration of being unable to complete the picture because a piece has been lost! The concept of a puzzle also seems to be appropriate, since learning is a puzzle and it is possible to create the big picture in many different ways and to start from different points.

Clearly, if learners are to have all the puzzle pieces in place there are very important implications for teachers. These are identified and presented in a complementary jigsaw puzzle identifying what is needed to enable learners to experience success. The learner puzzle and the teacher puzzle are colour co-ordinated to link explicitly the learner need to the teacher requirement.

I have been asked on occasion about the significance of the position of the individual pieces of the puzzle. Someone once suggested that the most important pieces should be at the corners, as he always starts with the corners when completing any jigsaw puzzle! This would require decisions to be made about the priority order of the pieces and makes the assumption that everyone begins jigsaw puzzles in the same way. It has also been suggested that numbering the pieces could be helpful. Again, a priority order would be needed and I believe that many of the pieces have equal importance and that it is difficult to take any one of them completely in isolation from the others. It is for those using the model to make decisions about any positioning or ordering of the pieces – it is, after all, a model and can therefore be adapted to suit the teachers/learners/school using it!

The model is made up of more than one layer. The top layer identifies the key principles that underpin successful learning. Further explanation of the terminology used to describe the elements of learning as they appear on the puzzle pieces is clearly necessary, and so the second layer provides more explicit detail.

The 'learner' puzzle is headed by the sentence starter:

To be a successful learner I need to ...

which then precedes each piece.

The 'teacher' puzzle is headed by the sentence starter:

To enable learners to be successful we need to ...

'We' is now used on this puzzle after development work with teachers clearly identified that this needs to be a collaborative, whole-school approach.

It is important to emphasize, however, that the real impact of the model comes from groups of individuals, such as staff teams, groups/classes of children, making independent interpretations of the model through engaging in discussion and debate about learning to deepen and share understanding. The examples included here are intended only to guide the development work of any group in creating their *own* second 'layer', which will reflect their interpretation of the key elements as stated on the top 'layer', and so create a powerful sense of ownership.

Even more important than the end product is the *process* of developing this second 'layer' – it is critical and central to the successful implementation of the model and subsequent practice. It is the process, after all, where significant discussion and debate is generated, and this contributes to deeper understanding and to the recognition of the need for consistency.

Further thinking behind the different pieces that make up the model and the explicit links between the 'learner model' and the 'teacher model' is offered on pages 32–43 as explanatory notes.

To be a successful learner I need to ...

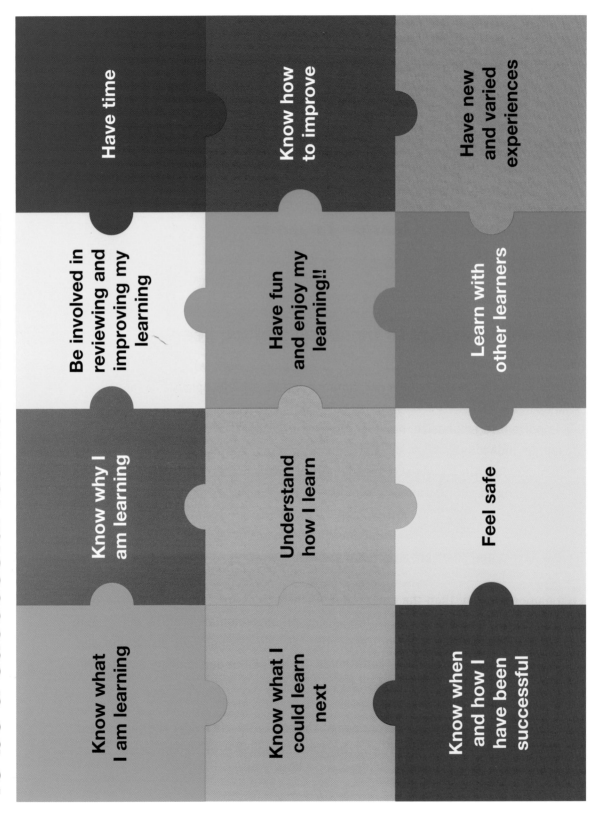

Have time

Know how to improve

Have new and varied experiences

Be involved in reviewing and improving my learning

Have fun and enjoy my learning!!

Learn with other learners

Know why I am learning

Understand how I learn

Feel safe

Know what I am learning

Know what I could learn next

Know when and how I have been successful

To be a successful learner I need to …

Know what the learning objective/intention is

Have it displayed, explained and discussed

Ask questions when I don't understand

Know what I have to do

Have a purpose for my learning

Know how it fits into the big picture

Know how my learning will help me make progress

Be able to use keys and codes

Learn strategies for recognizing my success and identifying what I need to improve

Learn the skills I need to evaluate my learning and progress

Talk to a friend

Ask questions

Think on my own and with a partner

See the big picture

Have helpful feedback from my teacher or my learning partner

Have time with my teacher when I need it

Know how to ask questions

Develop self-evaluation skills

Reflect on my learning:
- **on my own**
- **with a partner**
- **during the session**
- **at the end of a session**

Work with friends

Make choices and decisions

Use a wide range of tools and resources

Be prepared to have a go!

Know what my next step is

Know how to close my learning gaps

Understand my teacher's comments

Have high-quality examples and models

Understand success criteria

Show what I know

Show what I can do

Show what I understand

Say how I have been successful

Say how I can improve

'Check' in with my class/group

Feel confident to answer questions and offer ideas

Know it's OK to make mistakes

Ask for help

Have a learning partner for:
- **learning and listening**
- **talking and teaching**
- **sharing ideas**
- **helping and supporting**
- **encouraging**
- **having fun!**

Work:
- **on my own**
- **with a partner**
- **with my group**
- **with the whole class**
- **with older pupils**
- **with younger pupils**
- **with experts, coaches**

To enable learners to be successful we need to ...

Manage time effectively

Model desirable behaviours and effective learning strategies

Provide opportunities for learning in different ways

Provide focused feedback

Promote excellence and enjoyment

Provide opportunities for reflection and review

Share learning objectives, intentions and/or outcomes

Teach learners how to become self-evaluative

Create a safe environment

Produce clear explicit planning for learning

Ensure secure knowledge and understanding of the learning and of the learner

Have high expectations and set clear success criteria

To enable learners to be successful we need to …

- Plan for time to think and to talk with pupils about their learning
- Build in time for pupils to respond to feedback
- Provide time for questions, queries, ideas

- Provide pupils with models of high quality in:
  - social behaviours
  - learning behaviours
  - task outcomes
  - presentation of work
  - and so on

- Create opportunities for working individually, in pairs, in groups, with the whole class
- Vary teaching and learning styles and provide opportunities for pupils to exhibit learning in a range of styles

---

- Focus feedback on learning objectives
- Use constructive comments
- Identify strengths and points for improvement
- Use codes, symbols and 'close the gap' prompts
- Provide opportunities for self- and peer assessment

- Aspire towards excellence
- Reflect on current practice
- Model enjoyment of learning
- Have fun!
- (Enjoyment is the birthright of every child)

- Build in time during every lesson/session/day for individual, pairs or groups of pupils to:
  - think, talk or write about learning experiences
  - plan for improvement

- Display and discuss
- Elicit understanding from pupils
- Refer to objective/outcome during session
- Focus plenary on learning

- Provide opportunities for pupils to reflect on their learning
- Encourage focused talk about learning
- Use questions to engage learners in thinking about learning

---

- Negotiate codes and contracts for physical and emotional safety with pupils
- Model learner behaviour
- Model teacher as vulnerable learner!

- Have clear long-, medium- and short-term plans that identify intended learning outcomes for pupils

---

- Keep up to date with developments in subject/aspect
- Encourage pupils to ask questions
- Provide appropriate challenge and support

- Make accessible examples of successful high-quality outcomes
- Negotiate challenging criteria for success for individuals and groups
- Raise aspirations

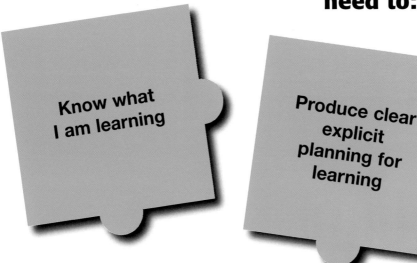

To be a successful learner I need to:

Know what I am learning

To enable learners to be successful we need to:

Produce clear explicit planning for learning

Explanatory notes

The most important purpose of planning is to provide clarity of the intended learning.

At the long-term stage this will be a curriculum framework or map that gives an overview of the breadth and balance of the whole curriculum over one or two years.

Medium-term plans (for example National Literacy and Numeracy Strategies and the QCA Schemes of Work) need to define the learning objectives in terms of knowledge, skills and understanding, with key activities identified as vehicles for the learning. It is important that there is some flexibility built into the plan, so that the adjustment and amendment of activities and tasks is facilitated to support learning and understanding.

Short-term plans need to identify clearly the learning objectives, the key points of the teacher input, differentiated activities, intended learning outcomes and key questions and, of course, resources and key vocabulary. Short-term plans need to be seen as 'work in progress' documents. No short-term plan should look the same on Friday afternoon as it did on Monday morning – it needs to be used for assessment notes so that teaching can be adjusted in the light of pupils' progress and understanding. Individuals who require additional support need to be recognized, as do those who consistently exceed the expected learning outcomes and therefore need extension and greater challenge to enhance their learning experiences.

To be a successful learner I need to:

To enable learners to be successful we need to:

Know why I am learning

Share learning objectives, intentions and/or outcomes

Explanatory notes

The sharing of learning objectives is essential to meaningful learning and is also key to the formative assessment process. Without understanding the planned objectives and/or outcomes of a task, learners are generally less focused and are occupied in an activity rather than engaged in learning. The arrival of the National Strategies for Literacy and Numeracy brought an expectation that teachers would share the learning objectives before each lesson; however, this is far more complex than simply displaying the objective as it appears in the teacher's plan. It requires the teacher to explain it, making it clear and explicit for the learners, to elicit understanding from the learners and to create opportunities for learners to seek further clarification, if necessary, before embarking upon the task. It is also important that the learning is placed in a wider context so that the pupils can see how their learning fits into a bigger picture.

Clearly, this is fundamental to all areas and aspects of learning, not simply to literacy and numeracy, though some teachers feel that it is less important for the non-core subjects, perhaps indicating a misunderstanding of the purpose behind the action.

Understanding the purposes for learning is fundamental to all learners and supports the move away from an activity-driven curriculum to one that is more learning oriented. The teacher needs to separate the learning from the task so that learners understand what it is they are learning and what it is they need to do.

To be a successful learner I need to:

To enable learners to be successful we need to:

Be involved in reviewing and improving my learning

Provide focused feedback

Explanatory notes

If learners are to know how well they have done, what their strengths are and what they need to do to improve, they require clear and focused feedback that is focused on the intended learning content and relevant to the individual learner. Research shows clearly that feedback is only valuable if it is used by the learner to make improvements and work towards raised achievement levels (Black and Wiliam, 1998; Black et al., 2002). It is important that it is based on shared and clearly communicated objectives for learning and reflects the criteria for success as defined by the teacher or, ideally, as negotiated with the learner.

The best feedback is oral – quality dialogue between teachers and learners and between learners and learners. Where feedback has to happen at a distance from the learner, it must be easily accessible and it is essential that time is given to the recipients of the feedback to ensure understanding and an opportunity to respond appropriately. The teacher needs to indicate where a learner has been successful, in such a way as to reinforce the learning. For example, using codes and symbols or highlighting are often more appropriate and effective strategies than a comment at the end of a piece of work.

If improvements are to be made, learners have to understand what it is they need to focus upon and, crucially, how the improvements can be made. It is of little use to say, for example, 'you need to be neater', 'improve your spelling', think about your 'layout' as this is not explicit and is likely either to be ignored or, worse still, to result in demotivation (see explanatory notes for 'know how to improve' on page 39).

To be a successful learner I need to:

To enable learners to be successful we need to:

Have time

Manage time effectively

Explanatory notes

How many times have we heard, or indeed voiced ourselves, comments such as 'that sounds an interesting idea, but we haven't got the time'. Since all the time available is already crammed with activity, this statement probably appears quite accurate. The drive for improvement seems relentless, and the pressure upon teachers and learners to cover a vast amount of content in order to meet the requirements of standardized tests and exams seems ever increasing, and yet in twenty-first-century education 'we are moving into a "learning economy" where success ... will reflect, more than anything else, the ability to learn' (OECD, 2001 quoted in Hargreaves, 2004).

We know that learning is a complex process that requires a significant investment of time if the learning is to be deep, meaningful and sustainable (Stoll et al., 2003). Taken in the context of the Successful Learner Model, the 'having time' as a learner is fundamental – time to talk, to listen, to develop understanding, to query and question and to think! Unfortunately the thinking time is the first thing to be left out in over-active (though not necessarily over-productive) classrooms. It is vital that teachers plan to provide learners with appropriate learning time and reduce the amount of time spent in completing activities. Many teachers become over-stressed and exhausted through trying to manage the curriculum. We need that pressure to be reduced so that teachers can concentrate on managing the learning. The new strategy for primary schools promises 'freedom and empowerment', and so hopefully should go some way to supporting teachers and enabling schools to become more creative learning communities.

To be a successful learner I need to:

To enable learners to be successful we need to:

Know what I could learn next

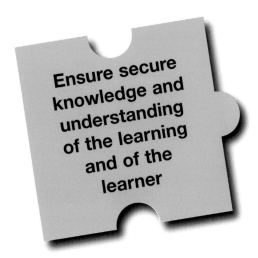

Ensure secure knowledge and understanding of the learning and of the learner

Explanatory notes

As learners we need to have a big picture, a sense of what we are aiming to learn and achieve and how it is relevant and meaningful to us. We also need to know how we are to get there, which direction to take and which landmarks are important. For every learner the feedback and guidance needed to make progress will vary, and the teacher therefore needs to have a good understanding of both the learning (subject knowledge, skills and so on) and the learner (preferred learning style, ability, disposition and so on).

It is vital that teachers provide appropriate challenge and support. For some learners who may find difficulty with a particular area of learning, it is important that each small step is made explicit to them so that they develop greater confidence. It may be that for others who have significant ability or strength in an area of learning, it is necessary to give a challenge or a problem to solve in order to move their learning on.

Feedback is essential if learners are to know what they need to do next and the key features of effective feedback have already been identified in the 'focused feedback' puzzle piece on page 34. This demonstrates clearly how all the pieces of this puzzle are interdependent and cannot be effective in isolation. What is also apparent is that there is no hierarchy or specific order of the pieces, though many discussions have taken place around which pieces are more or less important and which position each should assume. I cannot suggest a definitive order of importance, with the exception of the 'feel safe' piece, which must surely be in place first.

To be a successful learner I need to:

Understand how I learn

To enable learners to be successful we need to:

Teach learners how to become self-evaluative

Explanatory notes

Self-assessment and self-evaluation are both fundamental to successful learning. It is, however, important to distinguish between them. Self-assessment is about learning WHAT we have learned and self-evaluation is about learning HOW we learn. When learners self-assess, they are encouraged to review their progress and/or achievement in recent learning activities. To do this, learners revisit the learning objectives and success criteria for the learning activity and make a judgement about the extent to which these have been met. Self-evaluation is more than this – it requires the learner to analyse HOW they have learned and it involves skills that need to be taught specifically and developed over time.

The main emphasis of self-evaluation is thinking and articulating rather than the written response, though this is often appropriate. Teachers may choose a question and model a range of responses. For example: What really made you think? What did you find difficult? What helped you when something got tricky? What do you need more help with? What are you most pleased about? What have you learned that is new? How would you change the learning activity to suit another group?

There are many different strategies for developing self-evaluation skills: whole-class discussion, one-to-one reviews, working with a learning partner, graphic organizers and learning journals. The benefits of enabling learners to become self-evaluative are many: learners have increased self-esteem, recognize that difficulties herald new learning, identify with others who have similar problems, become more reflective, and thus learning improves.

To be a successful learner I need to:

To enable learners to be successful we need to:

Have fun and enjoy my learning!!

Promote excellence and enjoyment

Explanatory notes

'Enjoyment is the birthright of every child' says Charles Clarke in the foreword to the *Excellence and Enjoyment* document (DfES, 2003). We know that children and adults – indeed all learners – learn most effectively when they are motivated and engaged.

The new strategy for primary schools, *Excellence and Enjoyment*, stresses that teachers now have the power to make decisions about how they teach and that the National Curriculum and the National Strategies for Literacy and Numeracy need not be viewed as constraints but as a springboard for teaching. The goal is for every primary school to combine excellence in teaching with enjoyment of learning – and, of course, learners learn better when they are excited and engaged and where their learning is relevant and meaningful. The *Excellence and Enjoyment* document provides the principles of learning and teaching: 'Good learning and teaching should: ensure every child succeeds; build on what learners already know; make learning vivid and real; make learning an enjoyable and challenging experience; enrich the learning experience; promote assessment for learning.' The implementation of the Successful Learner Model addresses all these principles.

As human beings we have greatest recall of experiences that are important and meaningful in our lives. If, therefore, as teachers we wish learners to retain knowledge, skills and understanding, it is surely incumbent upon us to make the learning experiences as meaningful, relevant and enjoyable as possible. We now have a government strategy that advocates that 'good primary education is the fusion of excellence and enjoyment', so we need to discover what it is that our learners enjoy doing and how they enjoy learning, then we can aspire to excellence.

To be a successful learner I need to:

To enable learners to be successful we need to:

Know how to improve

Model desirable behaviours and effective learning strategies

Explanatory notes

Learners are often given information about what it is that they need to improve. They are less often given guidance on how to make the improvements. For the LEARN Project, conducted by the University of Bristol for QCA in 1999, over 200 students from Years 3 to 13 were interviewed 'to gain insights into their perceptions of themselves as learners and their understanding of how they think they learn best'. Many students had an understanding of what they had to do for individual tasks or problems, but were less sure about how this would lead to an improvement in their learning. This report also showed clearly that there was a significant dependency on the teachers and that in the main the students simply did what the teacher told them.

If learners are to become reflective, resourceful and, ultimately, independent and to be successful in the world, they must develop the necessary skills and behaviours. To be truly reflective it is important to be able to recognize one's strengths, identify areas for development and make the changes that bring about improvements. Teachers need to model the strategies and ways of working that will foster and develop this process, articulating exactly what they are doing and why. When the strategies and behaviours are understood and familiar practice to learners, the teacher can guide learners towards taking increased responsibility for their own improvements.

To be a successful learner I need to:

To enable learners to be successful we need to:

Know when and how I have been successful

Have high expectations and set clear success criteria

Explanatory notes

Whatever the age of the learner, there is always a need to recognize and enjoy the feeling of success. Motivation for learning is inextricably linked with success, which is itself often linked with external rewards. Understanding what is required to be successful and having success reinforced with positive feedback from teachers encourages more intrinsic motivation where the learner is rewarded by the sense of achievement that the experience of learning success brings in itself.

Learners need to understand the criteria for success that have been identified, or better still negotiated between teacher and learner, for any given task or learning activity. These may serve as a checklist for learners to use while completing a task to focus their thinking upon the key aspects of the learning (DfES, 2003). It is important that learners have examples of high-quality learning outcomes so that they understand the standards they are aiming for, so teachers' modelling and questioning techniques are of paramount importance.

The enthusiasm that teachers bring is significant in the motivation of learners. If teachers appear bored or disenchanted, it is likely that this will have a negative impact upon learners. It is also important that teachers communicate effectively the belief that everyone can be a learner – expectation whether high or low often becomes a self-fulfilling prophecy that can contribute to the self-concept of learners for life.

To be a successful learner I need to:

To enable learners to be successful we need to:

Feel safe

Create a safe environment

Explanatory notes

In order for effective learning to take place the climate in the learning environment must be physically and emotionally safe. Fear of failure has to be removed to encourage and develop honesty and openness. Learners need to be provided with support by being able to try out ideas and thinking in a warm, secure and unthreatening environment and by understanding that asking questions and making mistakes helps to advance new learning. It is important that all the needs of learners are valued – emotional and social, as well as academic.

Teachers need to spend time creating the learning environment with the learners, negotiating codes or contracts for physical and emotional safety. It is important that teachers model the appropriate behaviours for a safe learning environment and model themselves as vulnerable learners. To establish a learning community there must be a sense of ownership about the classroom culture, and each member of the community must feel valued. Any rewards should focus upon effort to promote risk taking and encourage learners to engage with rather than avoid difficult tasks.

The relationships that teachers have with their learners are fundamental to their ultimate success. Developing a safe and motivating learning environment takes time, energy and commitment, and, once established, needs tending and nurturing regularly so that all those within it can grow and flourish.

To be a successful learner I need to:

Learn with other learners

To enable learners to be successful we need to:

Provide opportunities for reflection and review

Explanatory notes

It is extremely valuable to enable personal reflection to play a strong role in learning sessions. All learners need to be encouraged to think about what they are achieving and how they are making progress, so that they may consider how they might do things differently in order to improve and what they might need to support them.

When we talk we are articulating our thinking. Talking our thoughts aloud or '"pole-bridging" ... is one of the most effective methods of enriching and accelerating learning' (Call and Featherstone, 2003). Even mature and successful learners talk to themselves when learning something new. Talking to a partner or a friend is always a feature of the 'movers' of learning; indeed, most of us work better when we can ask questions, seek reassurance and share ideas and concerns. There are great benefits to be gained from giving learners opportunity to talk together about their learning and to explain what they have learned and where they are finding difficulty.

Children who work regularly with a partner or with a small group also become better listeners and therefore more able to see a different point of view. They are more likely to take risks and engage in problem solving, since the stress of isolation has been removed. Focused talking together that is guided by the teacher can greatly enhance children's emotional literacy; they develop greater insight into the feelings of others and greater understanding of their own feelings enabling them to express themselves effectively and to work collaboratively.

To be a successful learner I need to:

To enable learners to be successful we need to:

Have new and varied experiences

Provide opportunities for learning in different ways

Explanatory notes

'Variety is the spice of life' may be a very old cliché, but it holds a significant truth. We know that a number of learning styles have been identified and studied over time; for example, the work of Gardner from 1983 on multiple intelligences and Kolb from 1984 on characteristic styles of learning. Personal experience also demonstrates clearly how significant it is to recognize individual preferences in how we learn. Although we fall mainly into four broad learning preferences – visual, aural, read/write and kinesthetic – it is important that teachers provide learners with experience of a range of styles, while acknowledging their own and their learners' preferred styles.

The role of the teacher is to facilitate learning, and this is enhanced when the learning is experiential and learners are actively involved in the learning process and have some control over its nature and direction (Rogers and Frieberg, 1994). Learners need to have opportunities to work individually, with a partner, as part of a learning team, and collaboratively as a member of a group or class, and to exhibit their learning using diverse styles and methods (see Critical Skills Programme on pages 87–88).

The learning pyramid overleaf shows that the more actively involved the learner is with the learning, the greater the learner's retention rate. In order to teach one needs to have a very clear understanding of the subject matter involved, thus the highest indicated rate on the pyramid is achieved when one is involved in teaching someone else.

Learning pyramid

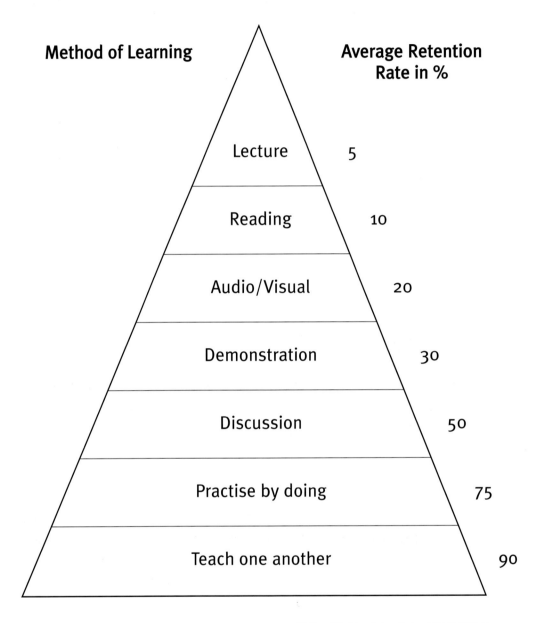

Method of Learning	Average Retention Rate in %
Lecture	5
Reading	10
Audio/Visual	20
Demonstration	30
Discussion	50
Practise by doing	75
Teach one another	90

(National Training Laboratories, Bethel, Maine)

Exploring the learning process

The three most important factors in learning are motivation, motivation and motivation.

Sir Christopher Ball

Defining learning

Currently, the term *learning* is very high profile. Many schools now claim to be committed to 'the learning agenda' (I think that one might reasonably question any school agenda that is not about learning!).

So what *is* learning? How can we define learning?

In this chapter I draw upon the work of a range of learning theorists to illustrate the thinking behind the development of the Successful Learner Model. I have attempted to make the links between the theory and the model more specific by representing the appropriate 'puzzle piece' in the margin close to the text to which it is connected (this is also done in Chapter 6). This has not been easy, since it is clearly not possible to take any piece in isolation from the others, as they are all connected to each other – hence it is the completed jigsaw puzzle that gives the whole picture. However, it may be helpful to think in particular about the identified pieces where they are indicated in the text and perhaps to think of other individual pieces that you might add or include.

For centuries people have thought, talked and theorized about learning. During the last 50 years, immense advances have been made and there is now a greater understanding of how learning happens. However, there is no single comprehensive theory and, indeed, such a theory may never exist, given the very complex nature of learning (Stoll et al., 2003).

In the past hundred years or so, many psychological theories about how people learn have appeared, all of which have yielded greater insight and understanding. For example:

> ➤ behaviourist theory – Skinner and Pavlov, who identified the power of reinforcement in learning

> ➤ constructivist theory and learning readiness – Piaget, whose theory placed action and self-directed problem solving at the heart of learning

> ➤ social constructivist theory – Vygotsky, whose work promoted the theory of learning as a social process.

Essential to the social constructivist theory of Vygotsky is the notion of the 'zone of proximal development', which is described as the distance between the actual development level of the individual engaged in problem solving in isolation and the level of potential where learners engage with new challenges supported and guided by adults and/or peers (Vygotsky, 1978).

Constructivism is a learning philosophy that suggests that we learn by constructing our own understanding of the world through reflection on our experiences and by adjusting our own mental models to accommodate new learning experiences. Social constructivism places great emphasis upon the importance of culture and, since we all develop in the context of a culture, this has a significant effect upon learning development. Social constructivism in classrooms is active and social and fosters the interdependence of teacher and learner and a collaborative classroom culture (Pollard and Triggs, 1997).

Theoretical perspectives on learning		
Behaviourist	**Constructivist**	**Social Constructivist**
visible behaviours	visible behaviours	visible behaviours
	physical and developmental contexts	physical and developmental contexts
		social and cultural contexts
Positivist	**Positivist/Interpretavist**	**Interpretavist**

s
u
r
f
a
c
e

d
e
e
p

(Raphael Reed, 2003)

It is clearly very important that, in order to reflect effectively upon practice, a clear understanding of what is meant by the term learning is required and this is not easy.

Know what
I am
learning

Know why
I am
learning

Be involved in
reviewing and
improving my
learning

Learning can be considered as the processes by which skills, attitudes, knowledge and concepts are acquired and understood, applied and used, or advanced and extended ... [It] should not be confused with mere completion of tasks.

(Pollard and Tann, 1990: 154)

Learning is usually taken for granted as a natural process. Indeed much of the time we are not aware that learning is taking place; it is only when we experience difficulties that we become aware of its complexity. So, what do we really know? We now have much more scientific knowledge about how the brain functions and we are just beginning to explore the implications of this understanding and the consequent impact upon learning. We know that learning is a social activity and is fundamentally about making connections.

Learning is intellectual, social and emotional. It is linear and erratic. It happens by design and by chance. We all do it and take it for granted, even though we do not have a clear understanding of what it means or how to make the most of it.

(Stoll et al., 2003: 24)

Learning through play

We know that early childhood development has a significant impact on how children learn. This is now acknowledged in the Foundation Stage Curriculum (DfES/QCA, 2000), which promotes learning through play. Primary schools talk frequently in terms of work and play, where the perception may be that 'work' is something that has to be done and may be 'hard' or 'difficult', whereas 'play' is fun and enjoyable and often a 'treat' that happens after 'work'. It may even be that the word 'work' has negative associations at home – perhaps adults at home are out of work, or do not like going to work and so an anxiety about work may be taken into school by very young children.

Having considered this use of language with early years teachers, where the words 'work' and 'play' have been replaced with the word 'learning', evidence suggests that the culture gradually changes.

Sandra Russ (2003), among others, has studied the significance of play in child development and her longitudinal studies looking at children's creativity over time suggest that imaginary play helps children to cope with stress in later life. Creative play, Russ states, enables children to 'play out their problems' giving them practice in problem solving. More creative six year olds often become better problem solvers by the age of 10. Russ has also found that 'the ability to be a good player is independent of a child's intelligence' and is more dependent upon the family environment and relationships. Creative play and collaborative play, therefore, need to be promoted so that children are getting valuable opportunities to develop the skills of co-operative play and the resilience that develops from early problem-solving experiences. Through playing with what is familiar, children will gradually develop an understanding of positive relationships and of how to make decisions and judgements. These skills and attitudes learned through creative play can be transferred to any learning situation.

Considering a learning culture

Children learn best through the smiling eyes of the teacher.

Professor Bart McGettrick (2002)

Professor Bart McGettrick, Glasgow University, talks of the nature of a 'learning culture'. He believes that education should be concerned with transformation, as a means of enabling citizens to develop as active participants in society.

A culture of learning has therefore got to raise issues about the purpose and nature of learning, and the place of both the individual and the community in this.

(McGettrick, 2002)

McGettrick suggests that 'learning cannot be narrowly defined, but consists of a hierarchy of learning' (2002). He articulates this 'learning hierarchy' thus:

Learning how to become

Learning how to be

Learning how to do

Learning how to learn

Learning how to repeat

Good education should address all aspects of learning, but should also place particular emphasis on the higher-order aspects. Most schools, however, concentrate more on learning how to repeat, to learn and to do, with a focus on outcomes and products. The higher elements of learning to be and learning to become are concerned with the personal and spiritual development of the individual, focusing more on relationships and processes, and are crucial in the development of a learning community. McGettrick (2002) describes the vision of citizenship as being 'based on … the development of attitudes and ways of thinking concerned with peace, and the care of self and others' requiring us to 'act responsibly and with a sense of mission for the improvement of society'.

This hierarchy of learning has some resonance with the now familiar hierarchy of needs formulated by Maslow. The basis of this theory is that we are all motivated by unsatisfied needs and that our lower-level needs, such as physical and emotional well-being, have to be met before higher-level needs, such as esteem and growth towards self-actualization. We are motivated to meet our most immediate need (Boeree, 1998); for example, someone who is experiencing family problems (belonging, love and security needs) will be less able to reach performance targets in their work (self-esteem and achievement needs) until these emotional needs are satisfied.

Maslow's Hierarchy of Needs (Maslow, 1943)

Clearly, then, it is crucial for us as educators that we identify and understand that the order and nature of needs may be different for different people at different times if learning experiences are to be meaningful and motivational.

This would seem to be highly relevant when considering the turbulent world in which our young people are growing up. Claxton, in his book *Building Learning Power* (2002), endorses this in exploring the question 'What is education for?'. He describes education as 'what societies provide for their young people to help them get ready to make the most of the world they are going to find themselves in'. The focus of this text is the development of learning 'power' through working on the four Rs of resilience, resourcefulness, reflectiveness and reciprocity.

Whatever terminology one uses, there can surely be little argument that young learners need to direct energy and enthusiasm into their learning, to learn in different ways through a range of experiences, to know themselves as learners and to relate positively to others in order to enable them to be confident and successful in a rapidly changing world.

Although more recently popularized by Goleman in his 1995 bestseller *Emotional Intelligence*, the term 'emotional intelligence' is relatively new in the world of education, but is rapidly becoming more high profile as schools recognize its potential in raising achievement. Emotional intelligence is also referred to as emotional literacy as it is about learning the language of emotions.

> *This language, when it is learned by the student, gives coping mechanisms to help them control their emotions, thoughts and behaviours. It does this by integrating emotion, thought and consciousness. This gives the individual greater insight into their own behaviour, and helps them choose actions which produce positive outcomes and feelings. It also gives the student planning skills and greater self-confidence to execute plans and achieve goals. For the student this results in higher self-esteem. It also reduces negative choices which lead to bad outcomes, feelings and low self-esteem.*

(Zimmerman, 1999)

Teachers play a hugely significant role in enabling children to expand '[their] emotional-social repertoire of understanding and reaction and so that children can learn from them [teachers] just by observing them' (Goleman, 2004). Preparing children for the future must be the mission of schools and this involves preparing them not simply to pass tests and examinations, but also to manage themselves and their emotions. Learning is inextricably linked with emotion. We all enjoy feeling good and this includes any learning situation in which we find ourselves. Emotions and feelings, one might argue, have greater influence upon our actions and our thinking than intelligence, so we cannot learn simply through the delivery of a curriculum. Think back to the best teacher you had as a child. It is almost certainly someone who made you feel special, treated you with respect, believed in your ability to succeed and made your learning interesting.

We are all learning all the time – most effectively when we are challenged, yet safe, and least effectively when we feel threatened. By understanding the significance of our emotions and recognizing that emotion is intrinsic to learning, we are better

Feel safe

Feel safe

Learn with other learners

Have fun and enjoy my learning!!

placed to create the optimum state for effective learning – 'relaxed alertness' – where challenge is balanced by a culture that encourages risk taking and promotes difficulty as part of the learning process (Caine and Caine, 1994).

Motivation, motivation, motivation!

Motivation concerns 'willingness to devote time to learning' (Stoll et al., 2003: 163), which requires commitment, openness and purpose if there is to be real subsequent learning. Motivation is often linked with external reward systems, which are often used in schools with the best of intentions. However, external or extrinsic motivation has significant implications for the development of learning.

> *Where the classroom culture focuses on rewards, 'gold stars', grades or place-in-the-class-ranking, then pupils look for the ways to obtain the best marks rather than at the needs of their learning which these marks ought to reflect. One reported consequence is that where they have any choice, pupils avoid difficult tasks.*

(Black and Wiliam, 1998: 8–9)

In the same situation as described by Black and Wiliam above, lower-attaining pupils often experience reinforcement of failure.

> *Many are reluctant to ask questions out of fear of failure. Pupils who encounter difficulties and poor results are led to believe that they lack ability, and this belief leads them to attribute their difficulties to a defect in themselves about which they cannot do a great deal. So they 'retire hurt', avoiding investing effort in learning which could only lead to disappointment, and try to build up their self-esteem in other ways.*

(Black and Wiliam, 1998: 9)

As already discussed the condition of 'relaxed alertness' is ideal for learning and risk taking, whereas lower-attaining pupils, who believe that they are unable to succeed, experience significant stress when confronted by any new learning or challenge. This can lead to 'learned helplessness', where the learner either chooses a simple task where success is virtually guaranteed, or opts out of the challenging situation. This may be through exhibiting a lack of interest or understanding or through inappropriate behaviour that draws the attention of the teacher away from the learning to the issue of behaviour.

However, where the culture in the classroom is emotionally safe, encourages effort and is supportive of the self-determination of the individual, it is likely that pupils will become more intrinsically motivated to succeed. Intrinsic motivation comes from within, and is much more successful in improving the quality of learning. Intrinsically motivated pupils want to learn, explore and understand for the sense of achievement that the experience of learning brings in itself, rather than for any external reward. Intrinsically motivated learning is far more likely to be meaningful and lifelong. This is only achievable if the school is a real learning environment, which focuses on individual learners, 'stimulating their intrinsic interest ... and providing them with the direction and confidence that they need to succeed' (Stoll et al., 2003).

Developing motivation for learning is extremely complex, since there are many vital components. The diagram shown overleaf attempts to represent the complexity.

The significance of learner self-esteem and its impact on achievement is now recognized and acknowledged by most schools, and indeed frequently appears in vision statements or core purposes. According to the Assessment Reform Group, however, this is but one essential component. It is vital that all the partners in learning have a shared understanding of these terms and how they impact upon learning.

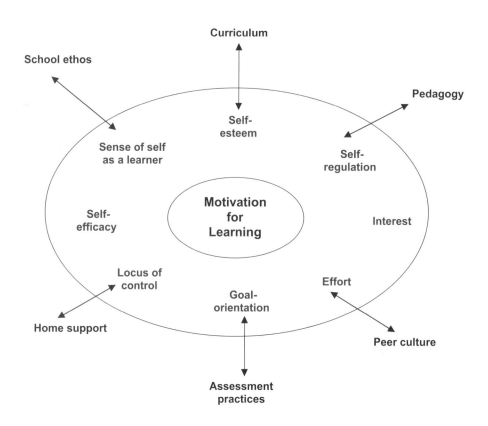

Self-esteem	how one values oneself as a person and as a learner
Self-efficacy	how capable one feels of succeeding in a learning task
Self-regulation	the capacity to evaluate one's own work and to make choices about what to do next
Goal-orientation	whether one's goal is to learn in order to understand or to perform well on a test (which may not reflect secure learning)
Interest	the pleasure from engagement with learning
Effort	how much one is prepared to try and persevere
Locus of control	how much one feels in control of learning as opposed to its being directed by others
Sense of self as a learner	how confident one feels of being able to learn from the classroom experiences provided

Based on a systematic review of research by Harlen and Deakin Crick (2003).

The main focus of the Assessment Reform Group review was to explore the impact of testing on pupil motivation for learning and, not surprisingly, this is largely negative, although the impact varies in degree with the characteristics of the learners and the conditions of the learning. There is great emphasis placed upon what can be done to minimize this negative impact and implications for the work of teachers is helpfully identified in lists with sub-headings 'do more of this' and 'do less of this':

Do more of this ...	And do less of this ...
➤ Provide choice and help pupils to take responsibility for their learning	➤ Define the curriculum in terms of what is in the tests to the detriment of what is not tested
➤ Discuss with pupils the purpose of their learning and provide feedback that will support the learning process	➤ Give frequent drill and practice for test taking
➤ Encourage pupils to judge their work by how much they have learned and by the progress they have made	➤ Teach how to answer specific test questions
➤ Help pupils to understand the criteria by which their learning is assessed and to assess their own work	➤ Allow pupils to judge their work in terms of scores or grades
	➤ Allow test anxiety to impair some pupils' performance (particularly girls and lower-performing pupils)
➤ Develop pupils' understanding of the goals of their work in terms of what they are learning; provide feedback to pupils in relation to these goals	➤ Use tests and assessment to tell students where they are in relation to others
➤ Help pupils to understand where they are in relation to learning goals and how to make further progress	➤ Give feedback relating to pupils' capabilities, implying a fixed view of each pupil's potential
➤ Give feedback that enables pupils to know the next steps and how to succeed in taking them	➤ Compare pupils' grades and allow pupils to compare grades, giving status on the basis of test achievement only
➤ Encourage pupils to value effort and a wide range of attainments	➤ Emphasize competition for marks or grades among pupils
➤ Encourage collaboration among pupils and a positive view of each others' attainments	

(Harlen and Deakin Crick, 2003)

Literature on motivation often talks of *motivation orientation* and describes pupils as being oriented towards both a need for success and a need to avoid failure (Dweck and Leggett, 1988). Some pupils select tasks that are difficult and then persist with the challenge of completing them, while others select simple tasks where they are confident of success. The former could be said to be *learning-goal oriented*, whereas the latter could be said to be *performance-goal oriented*. Pupils who are learning-goal oriented are more likely to be high achievers since they are more likely to engage in activities that are challenging. Pupils who are performance-goal oriented are more concerned with avoiding failure and therefore often engage in very simple activities, which minimize the potential for and the interest in learning.

'Motivation is emotion in motion' (Smith, 2003) – if we focus upon enabling pupils to learn in a state of 'relaxed alertness' (Caine and Caine, 1994), they are more likely to become *learning-goal oriented, lifelong learners.*

Know what
I am learning

Know how
to improve

Have fun
and enjoy my
learning!!

Putting the principles into practice: case studies

The following case studies describe how the Successful Learner Model has been introduced, implemented and developed in some of the zone schools of Success@ Excellence in Cities Action Zone, and it is with their kind permission that I have been able to include a range of photographs and examples that illustrate their practice.

Case study A

The headteacher of Fair Furlong Primary School describes the developing process of introducing and implementing the Successful Learner Model as 'organic and responsive to change'. He believes that there is now a growing capacity within the senior management team to begin to unpick the barriers to learning and to develop a strategy for building learning potential and a common language of learning. The senior management team of the school has developed a peer coaching process from the model that has involved all the teachers and secured a move towards greater 'in house' professional development opportunities and experiences. Initially, teachers worked together in small teams to select a piece of the 'puzzle' as a specific area for development, and from this they set 'smart' (specific, measurable, achievable, realistic, time-constrained) targets. These were then used subsequently as foci for observation and review and to inform future improvement planning. The first phase of the peer coaching has been completed, and where successful, the headteacher has reported significant improvements in classroom practice.

The headteacher explained that teachers who were already reflective practitioners have 'flown' with their understanding, interpretation and implementation of the model, and that all the teachers are further developing reflective skills through interrogating the model and engaging in dialogues focused upon learning and working more collaboratively with more reflective colleagues. He believes that this may well result from the simplicity of the model, as it is easily accessible.

In this school the model has been introduced to all the children and developed by individual teachers using a variety of strategies, including digital photographs with the youngest classes and interactive displays and presentations from some of the older children. When asked what impact he thought there had been upon the children, the headteacher explained that this varied from class to class depending on the extent to which the model has been used with the children.

> *Where there has been most impact children are articulate about themselves as learners. They take responsibility for their learning, can articulate what they are learning and why and where they need to make improvements.*

(Headteacher)

Earlier this year a senior school improvement officer from the local education authority visited the school and asked children from Years 5 and 6 about their learning. One boy responded:

> *We are learning how to improve our writing by using more interesting words and phrases. We are helping each other by highlighting the really good phrases which have lots of description, and improving a phrase which is not so good – like this one here (pointing at a specific phrase in writing) – and here is the better phrase that I'm going to use.*

(Year 6 pupil)

I have worked closely with the Year 6 teacher for over three years, and she has made extremely valuable contributions to the development of the model. She has asked questions, offered suggestions and challenged my ideas. I have benefited greatly from her skills and expertise. She describes learning as the priority in her teaching, both for her and for her pupils. She is confident and secure in her own skills and abilities and has used the model with colleagues to bring together all the strategies that work well. She reports that children are more engaged in their own learning, particularly when learning with a partner, are recognizing and enjoying their successes and are beginning to identify where they need to go next in their learning, and that teaching is easier, less stressful and more fun!

Why have learning partners?

This Year 6 class had been working with learning partners for two terms when they were asked about the benefits to them as learners. They were given the following two questions:

- What does an effective learning partner do?

- What does an effective learning partner say?

Below are the collated responses of the group.

What does an effective learning partner do?	What does an effective learning partner say?
➤ Helps you to learn and makes it more fun ➤ Helps you get your ideas out ➤ Makes it interesting ➤ Listens to you ➤ Helps you to focus on your work ➤ Gives you help if you are stuck ➤ Makes you full of enthusiasm	➤ Do you need help? ➤ That is good work, well done ➤ You could do something to improve ➤ That work could be neater

When asked about the impact that working with the model had had upon the children, she explained that she had been developing parts of the jigsaw before it was produced in its current format through focused assessment for learning strategies:

> *The children I taught at the time made incredible progress in their learning. They loved coming to school, were focused, relaxed and really appreciated this way of learning. The SATs results were greatly improved from previous years.*

She is confident that working with the model will be even more effective with her new class as the children have already had some experience with their previous teacher. Concerning the future, she hoped that teachers would become more confident, reflective practitioners with the Successful Learner Model being an everyday part of high-quality teaching, and that the school would become a place where pupils and teachers share a common language of learning.

I asked four Year 6 pupils how the jigsaw helps with their learning:

> *Well, if someone came in off the street into our class, they could look at the jigsaw and by the end of the day they would know what to do.*

(Nina)

> *It tells us what we need to do to be successful learners and it tells Miss what to do to be a successful teacher, so it helps us all.*

(Katherine)

> *It (the jigsaw) fits together and if you don't have all the pieces it won't fit together properly.*

(Anna)

> *The success criteria tell you what you should know how to do by the end of the lesson.*

(Dean)

A Year 2 teacher considers that the Successful Learner Model supports and enhances modern learning theory and redefines the roles of the teacher and the learner. She feels that its accessibility enables teachers to explore the fundamental principles of effective learning that underpin the practice.

With a significantly high number of children with special educational needs (SEN) in her class, she created an environment and opportunities for the children where learning skills have taken precedence over curriculum delivery. She negotiated with other teachers in Key Stage 1 to concentrate on the puzzle piece 'Know what I am learning' as this was considered to be fundamental to changing the nature of teaching in Key Stage 1 by moving from 'what are we going to do?' to 'what are we going to learn?'. This was put into practice by building it into the short-term planning and adding a box that states 'We are learning ...'.

This proved to be quite challenging for some staff who were more familiar with explaining activities to the children. After six weeks the teachers reviewed what was happening and found that it was only the most able children who could articulate what they were *learning*. Agreeing that the teacher is responsible for all the children to know what they are learning, further kinesthetic strategies were put in place to focus on this in the classroom. Children repeated what they were learning, stood up and chanted what they were learning. Six weeks later the teachers observed that children were beginning to be able to articulate what they had learned (see photograph on page 63) and what they were learning to do:

> *There was a massive improvement in the quality of what the children were experiencing on a daily basis, because their whole day had moved from a series of things to do to what they were supposed to be learning. We also have a success criteria box on our planning so that, to support the teacher who is finding it harder, there is a structure for ideas on what the success criteria might be. And the fact that these conversations are going on means that when you talk to children about what is going on and what has happened, they can actually say something meaningful ... it's had an enormous impact on them.*

(Year 2 teacher)

Drawing upon her personal experience this teacher articulated her thinking about how real engagement with learning reduces the incidence of inappropriate behaviour in the classroom. She has found that children who feel valued and understand what is expected of them, generally behave well, and this has been observed in the Key Stage 1 classes since more work focusing on learner needs, derived from the Successful Learner Model, has been implemented.

As a skilled coach, she feels that the implementation of the Successful Learner Model and the peer coaching process has raised awareness of the key learning and teaching skills and helped to change the language of the school, so that it is now about learners and their learning. She feels that the priority is to enable individuals to become independent learners who are socially competent in a school:

> *Where learning is really being understood and being embraced by the majority of people as something which is a positive experience and something where we all fail and succeed daily.*

(Year 2 teacher)

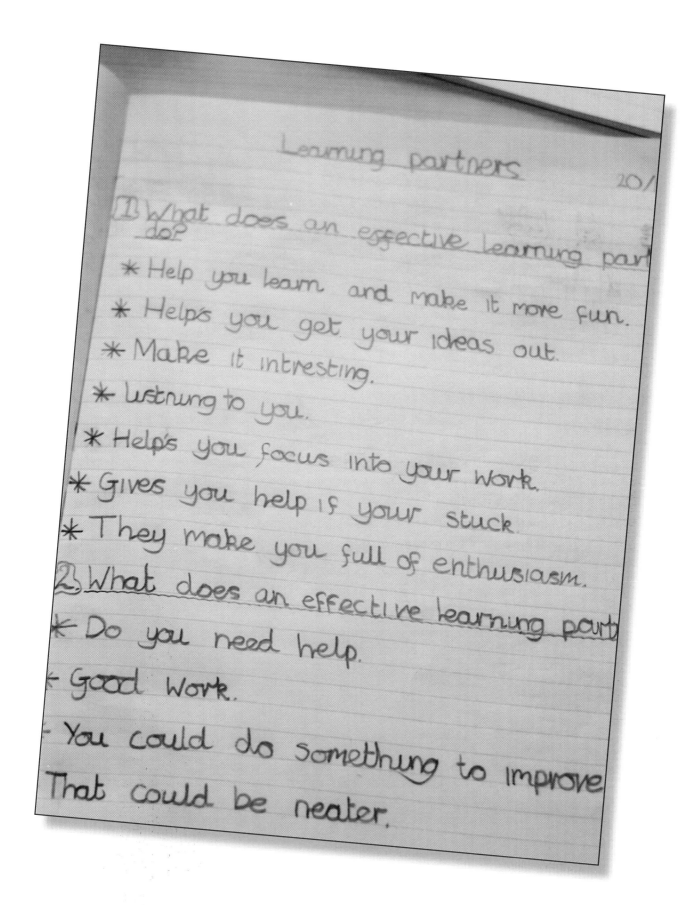

Learning partners   20/

①What does an effective learning part
   do?
   * Help you learn and make it more fun.
   * Helps you get your ideas out.
   * Make it intresting.
   * listning to you.
   * Help's you focus into your work.
   * Gives you help if your stuck.
   * They make you full of enthusiasm.
②What does an effective learning part
* Do you need help.
- Good work.
- You could do something to improve
That could be neater.

Case study B

In Headley Park Primary School the model has been introduced into all Key Stage 1 and 2 classes and I have facilitated follow-up sessions for staff to explore the impact and share their experiences. The staff conducted an 'audit' of practice across the school. They identified certain 'pieces of the puzzle' that they felt were well embedded in their practice and reported that after exploring their understanding of the principles embraced by the model, they had an increased awareness of the areas that they considered they needed to develop further. These were, in particular, effective feedback practice and strategies for promoting independent learning, which they see as fundamental to raising achievement, particularly of their more able learners. The senior management team has ensured that this is an identified priority focus in the school development plan for next year.

In school B, I gave a class of Year 6 children the challenge to create their own 'second layer' of the puzzle. The teacher first explained to the class that the session was going to focus upon what they thought about learning and their interpretation of the jigsaw pieces and that there were no 'right and wrong' answers. Most of the children became engaged in conversation immediately and I observed that relevant, focused discussion was taking place in each of the six groups. Each group was asked to consider six pieces of the puzzle, brainstorm their ideas and then decide on what to record. The children produced careful and considered statements in addressing their puzzle pieces. For example, when considering why time is needed for successful learning the responses included: 'Know how much time there is; pace yourself, have time to talk to the teacher and other learners; leave time to check and improve' (Year 6 written response).

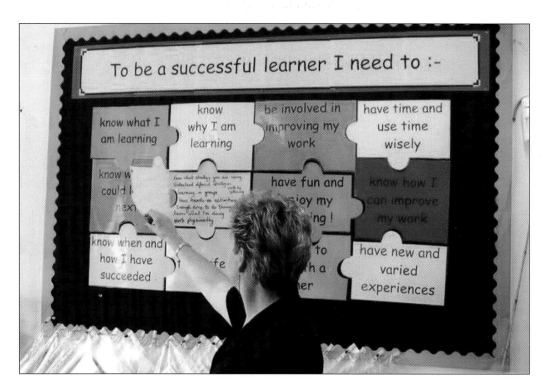

The class puzzle in this case has been enlarged to become a wall display where the top layer can be removed to reveal the second layer created by the children. This second layer is written on laminated card using a non-permanent pen so that the language may be changed as appropriate to the developing understanding and maturity of the learners.

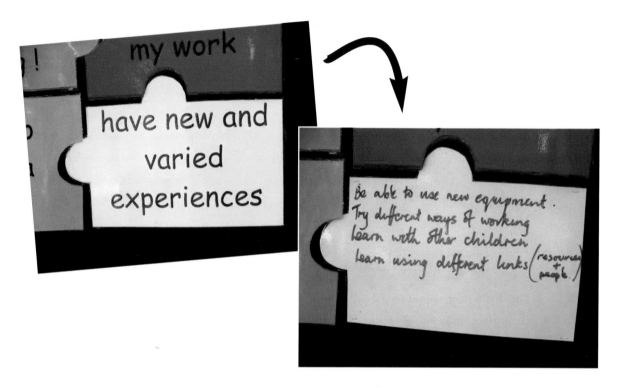

The class teacher asked the children what improvements he could make to support their learning. He has since used the thinking of his pupils to inform what he needs to do next to meet their independently identified learning needs and to further develop their key learning skills.

It was felt, as a result of the high quality of the 'jigsaws' produced by pupils in these primary schools, that the partner secondary schools needed to be aware of the depth of understanding their prospective Year 7 pupils already had. A twilight session was held where members of staff from the primary and secondary schools met with upper Key Stage 2 pupils, who were happy to share their understanding and ideas. The children explained the puzzles to the secondary staff, who were clearly interested in how they were used in their classrooms and were very impressed by pupils' knowledge and understanding of learning.

Keeping learners engaged and motivated is key to their learning success (Clarke, 2001; Stoll et al., 2003). It was apparent, from the confidence demonstrated by these pupils, that they had been learning in a safe environment where they were supported and valued by their peers and teachers. They were excited and eager to talk about what they had been doing, 'proud to share what they know and can do with others' (Stoll et al., 2003).

The headteacher of one of the secondary schools commented upon how well the Successful Learner Model dovetails with the new Ofsted framework that now focuses specifically on the quality of learning. He stated that it is no longer good enough just to have high-quality teaching – the quality of learning needs to be high too. He believes that the model will help to address the attitudinal issues around learning and feels that if primary schools are already beginning to have such dialogue, it is definitely something for secondary colleagues to build upon.

Case study C

In Highridge Infant School, the model was introduced to all the staff – teachers, learning support assistants and nursery nurses – on a professional development day. Staff then worked together in their planning teams to determine how to implement the key principles effectively and appropriately with very young children. In the Foundation Stage it was decided to focus upon enabling the children to identify what they are learning through the varying activities and routines in the classroom, and the following key learning intentions were introduced to the children:

- ➤ We are learning to listen.
- ➤ We are learning to make friends and help each other.
- ➤ We are learning to look after our things.
- ➤ We are learning to share and take turns.
- ➤ We are learning to talk with others.
- ➤ We are learning to do things for ourselves.

Each of these statements became the focus of an individual puzzle piece, and as these were introduced to the children, photographs were taken to illustrate some examples of appropriate learning behaviours. The children engaged in a variety of teacher-led activities that helped them to focus upon their learning and to begin to identify learning behaviours.

The Nursery teacher believes that developing the Successful Learner Model has had a 'twofold benefit' to the learning and teaching in the Nursery:

> *We have had to have a very clear focus on what the children are learning and on what we need to do as teachers to facilitate that learning. It is so easy to drift into an activity-based curriculum, but this is closely linked to the Reggio Emilia approach and maintains a focus on learning.*

The process of creating the class jigsaw has required all the Foundation Stage staff to focus upon the positive behaviours that they wish to promote and to enable the children to recognize themselves as 'good' learners. The staff team is developing greater use of a consistent 'learning' vocabulary.

The annotated photographs that make up the class puzzle have drawn the attention of the parents too, who, in addition to having the pleasure of seeing their children in the photographs, are also beginning to recognize the value of all the learning that is taking place in the classroom rather than focusing purely upon the academic elements of their child's education.

In Key Stage 1, the teaching and learning support staff decided to focus on six puzzle pieces: five drawn from the original puzzle with the addition of a piece entitled 'know that I am a learner' as they felt strongly that very young children need to recognize themselves as competent learners. These puzzle pieces are represented in a table on pages 70 and 71.

The Year 1 teacher began by asking her children what they thought makes a good learner. She feels that the taking of their ideas and identifying the specific actions that illustrate high-quality learning behaviours has had the biggest impact on the children since they recognized how they could become successful learners themselves. The children are now more able to identify what they have been learning in the plenary session, rather than simply recalling what they have done.

Since high-quality talking and listening feature in all aspects of learning, it became important that the children could recognize for themselves when talk is helpful and when it is not. Working in small groups they discussed and listed types of helpful talk and unhelpful talk. They produced a most comprehensive list which is now represented as a classroom wall display and features 'Mr Chatterbox'!

The Year 1 teacher feels that her children have gained a greater understanding of what it is to be a learner and are beginning to take more responsibility for their actions and behaviours:

> *We need to focus more in Key Stage 1 on getting the learning behaviours established and what it means to be a good learner. This provides firm foundations for learning for life. It is important that the time spent developing positive learning behaviours is valued by everyone, beginning with the leadership of the school.*

Key Stage 1 teachers and learners concentrated on the six pieces shown on page 70.

They then followed the development of the model and created a 'second layer' of their puzzle that describes the specific actions involved for each piece of their puzzle (see page 71). The teachers and learning support staff developed the second layer for their puzzle with the children. It describes the specific actions involved for each piece of their puzzle.

The staff then worked together to create a two-layer puzzle that illustrates what needs to happen in order to enable successful learning to take place as per the model, but again developing it themselves through discussion in order to establish a true sense of ownership (see pages 72 and 73).

To be a successful learner I need to ...

Know that I am a learner	Have time	Feel safe
Have fun and enjoy my learning	Have new and varied experiences	Learn with other learners

To be a successful learner I need to …

Listen and watch carefully

Feel comfortable to ask questions

Show others what I can do

Want to learn

Feel happy

Have choices about what I do

Make friends

Play nicely

Be praised when I try hard

Be happy to try new things

Time to:

Talk

Finish my tasks

Watch and practise

Think about what I have learned

Be active and time to be quiet

Have lots of different opportunities for learning

Learn through what interests me

Have access to a range of resources

Have access to both inside and outside learning areas

Be able to learn in different ways

Be able to develop my own ideas

Have clear boundaries

Have space

Trust the adults

Have routine

Be able to say how I feel

Be part of a friendly learning community

Take part

Talk and listen

Share and take turns

Have caring adults guiding and supporting me

Know I can ask for help from adults or other children

To enable learners to be successful we need to …

Explain purpose of activities/what it is hoped children will learn	Plan time effectively	Create a safe learning environment
Promote excellence and enjoyment	Provide a wide range of relevant learning opportunities across all areas of learning	Provide opportunities for reflection and review

To enable learners to be successful we need to ...

Plan opportunities that cater for different learning styles

Allow children to initiate their own learning

Give high priority to promoting self-esteem and a positive disposition to learning

Value children's achievements

Provide a stimulating, happy learning environment

Celebrate children's learning and give positive encouragement

Provide motivating experiences that will develop curiosity and persistence

Ensure children experience a sense of success

Praise children's efforts and behaviour, saying why the praise is being given

---

Plan time to allow for observations of and interactions with individual children

Plan a daily routine that allows children to make choices, sustain interest and reflect on their experiences

Engage with children, listening to and giving time to communicate their ideas and responses

Provide learning opportunities that reflect and build on children's strengths and interests

Provide opportunities to work independently, in a small group or in a large group

Provide a balance of child-initiated and adult-led experiences

Ensure children have access to all areas of learning both inside and outside

Provide learning areas that are well resourced and accessible

---

Acknowledge children's feelings, respond sensitively and give reassurance as needed

Ensure all children receive individual attention

Value all children and their families

Listen to and recognize children's ideas and ensure children's rights are respected

Encourage children to take risks and ensure that they feel safe to make mistakes

Provide a routine that reflects order and flexibility

Ensure children feel they are valuable members of the learning community and feel a sense of belonging

Plan opportunities for children to talk freely with adults and other children about their play/activity

Model reflection on experiences

Create stimulating, purposeful learning areas for co-operative play

Provide opportunities for working collaboratively

Case study D

Teyfant Community School is a large primary school where the staff and children have been developing the Successful Learner Model since 2003. Building on the improvement in the quality of teaching in the school, the headteacher and senior management team decided that the time was right to turn their attention to the quality of learning with a focus on assessment for learning. This initiative was given high priority from the outset and with significant professional time dedicated to the introduction and subsequently the development of the model.

After exploring their understanding of successful learning as staff, each class developed their own interpretation of successful learning, which led to class displays based on the Successful Learner Model and retaining the concept of the jigsaw puzzle.

The photographs that follow illustrate the interpretations of all the age groups from the Foundation Stage through to Year 6 classrooms.

Foundation Stage

Year 1

Year 2

Year 3

Year 4

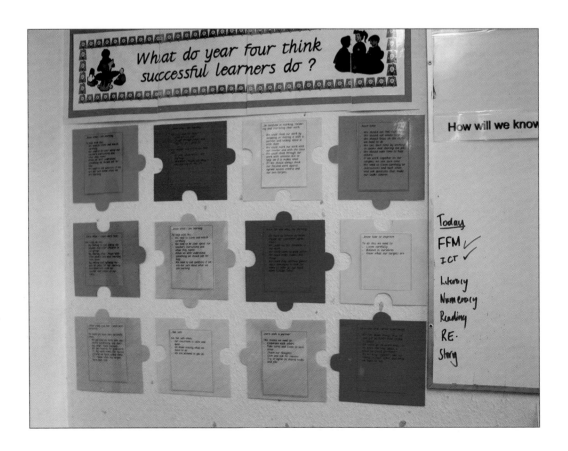

Years 5 and 6 (using the original Successful Learner Jigsaw format)

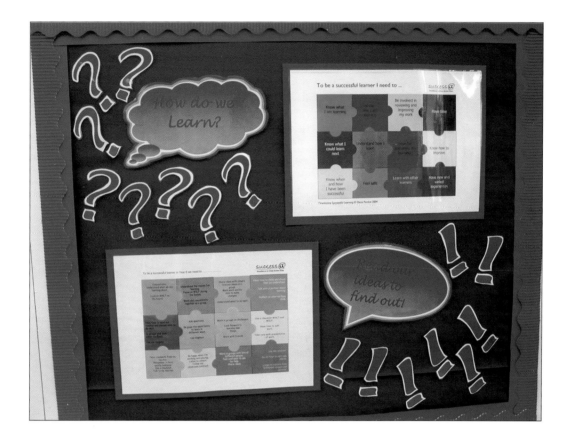

To enable learners to be successful at Teyfant we need to …

Plan for long, medium + short term in discussion with colleagues clearly identifying intended learning outcomes for pupils.

Be prepared with quality resources.

Have knowledge of the subject I am teaching.

Provide verbal + visual explanation of lesson objectives. Revisit objectives throughout the lesson.

Ensure children can explain their understanding of the learning.

Model learning.

Provide consistent verbal + written feedback, focused on the learning objective.

Give children opportunities to reflect on learning.

Provide feedback which clearly explains the next step.

Create a sense of self-worth and achievement.

Be well prepared for lessons and plan for time to think and talk.

Have a structured timetable that allows for flexibility.

Have effective lines of communication with all staff.

Encourage pupils to ask questions.

Keep up to date with developments in subject/aspect.

Ensure a child centred approached.

Receive quality feedback on planning.

Provide opportunities for pupils to reflect on their learning.

Encourage focused talk about learning.

Use questions to engage learners in thinking about learning.

Promote a curriculum so that all children can experience success.

Create a quality environment where it's 'cool to learn'.

Reflect on current practice (smiling children and staff are proud of our school).

Model and apply consistent routines.

Show care and respect.

Provide high-quality models of learning outcomes.

Have clear, consistent and shared expectation across the school.

Engage learners appropriately with objectives + success criteria.

Create challenging and achievable expectations.

Provide a welcoming environment where all individuals share a sense of belonging.

Ensure that learners feel emotionally safe + confident to take risks.

All have understanding of the 3Bs (be safe, be responsible, be respectful).

Plan and manage time effectively for:
● Reflection
● Questioning
● Using tools and varied strategies e.g. collaborative working

Vary groupings.

Use a variety of learning styles and teaching styles.

Make effective use of experiences in school and at home.

Use a variety of media and products.

The teaching and learning support staff have also worked together to create their own Successful Learner Model from the teaching perspective, identifying what needs to happen to enable successful learning to take place (see page 80).

The school has identified the impact of developing this initiative on teaching and on learning.

Impact on teaching (so far...!):

➤ Whole-school agreement

➤ High profile of learning

➤ Modified planning

➤ Identified and shared learning intentions and success criteria

➤ Prompts for learning

➤ Varied learning experiences

➤ Increased awareness of the importance of quality questioning

➤ Importance of nature of feedback.

Impact on learning (so far...!):

➤ Children's own understanding of successful learning made clearer

➤ Children using learning prompts independently

➤ Using the model* has led to an increase in progress – clearly visible to children (and teachers)

➤ Children are clearer about their next steps

➤ Children say they feel more involved in their learning and that the model* helps them to keep motivated.

The model continues to evolve and will develop in different ways in different schools, since the process of working with the ideas encompassed by the model need to be organic. The feedback I have already received from teachers and learners has contributed to interim reviews of the model and resulted in changes being made. Hopefully, this will mean that the model becomes more accessible and more useful since it will reflect the thinking of more teachers and learners.

* Model – the individual class interpretation, where all class members have ownership.

Know when and how I have been successful

Be involved in reviewing and improving my learning

Know what I could learn next

6 Learning our way forward

The important thing is not so much that every child should be taught, as that every child should be given the wish to learn.

Sir John Lubbock, the First Lord Avebury (1834–1913)

Reflecting upon my own experience of school, I can honestly say that I do not recall feeling successful. I remember working very hard and being constantly disappointed that I had not done as well in tests and assignments as many of my peers. I found maths very difficult and constantly felt highly anxious as my teacher found it irritating that I did not understand and often made my inadequacy public. School reports convinced me that I was very average and not likely to be a high achiever – I have very strong memories of the attention and special treatment given to those students who were likely to gain entrance to the universities of Oxford and Cambridge. This experience meant that in the early years of my teaching career I was deeply concerned that perhaps I would not be 'good enough'. Gradually, I discovered that I had some talent for engaging children in their learning; I felt successful and my self-belief increased.

Much time and energy has been devoted to improving the quality of teaching during the last ten plus years, with significant success. The challenge now is to focus upon developing and improving learning skills and dispositions in order to raise achievement in its broadest sense and to prepare young people for life in the twenty-first century.

The reforms of recent years have focused largely on standards and structures. These are important – standards especially; but they have almost nothing to say about whether the system can help students become capable of meeting the more complex demands that will be made upon them in the future.

(Bayliss quoted in Stoll et al., 2003: 17)

The significance of assessment for learning

➤ Why is it that at the end of the day the teachers crawl out of school while the children skip out?

➤ Who is tired out?

➤ Who has been doing all the work?

We need to develop a classroom culture where learners are expected to take responsibility for their learning, coached and facilitated by teachers; a culture where skills, behaviours and attitudes are recognized as having equal value with the acquisition of knowledge; a culture where everyone is a learner. In such a culture, the curriculum becomes a framework that supports teaching and learning, underpinned by secure pedagogical understanding.

In *How to Improve your School*, Brighouse and Woods (1999) discuss the significance of a teaching and learning policy. They suggest that in successful schools the staff work together to create a policy that emphasizes a shared philosophy, incorporating core values and beliefs, and a shared language. Central to such a policy are the key issues of teaching and learning; for example, teaching skills, teaching and learning styles, resources, professional development and monitoring, review and evaluation strategies.

By 1998 the research work of Black and Wiliam (King's College, London) was beginning to gather momentum and attract attention. They were placing great emphasis on the importance of formative assessment and suggesting that this was the key to raising achievement through enabling learners to take greater responsibility for their learning, to become active participants rather than passive recipients and, thereby, to experience learning success. Formative assessment is integral to learning and teaching processes, whereas summative assessment measures what has been learned.

Shirley Clarke (2001) uses a gardening analogy to define the two main forms of assessment:

> *If we think of our children as plants, summative assessment of the plants is the process of simply measuring them. The measurements might be interesting to compare and analyse, but in themselves do not affect the growth of the plants. Formative assessment, on the other hand, is the garden equivalent of feeding and watering the plants – directly affecting their growth.*

The drive to raise standards and the burdens of testing and recording attainment have contributed to a reduction in the quantity and the quality of interactions in the classroom, and in this situation the role of formative assessment or assessment for learning becomes marginalized. While acknowledging that summative assessment is essential in terms of making judgements about achievement, it is vital that the potential of formative assessment in raising achievement is recognized. Therefore, there is clearly a need to reconcile the tensions that exist between them.

> *Assessment for learning is any assessment for which the first priority in its design and practice is to serve the purpose of promoting pupils' learning. It thus differs from assessment designed primarily to serve the purposes of accountability, or of ranking, or of certifying competence.*
>
> *An assessment activity can help learning if it provides information to be used as feedback, by teachers, and by their pupils, in assessing themselves and each other, to modify the teaching and learning activities in which they are engaged. such assessment becomes formative assessment when the evidence is actually used to adapt teaching to meet learning needs.*

(Black et al., 2002)

In order to raise achievement, learners need above all to be intrinsically motivated by a desire to learn, and this requires them to be actively involved in their learning. Key features of being actively involved in learning include:

a clear understanding of the learning objective and outcome

time for reflection and review

opportunities to make improvements

the celebration of success.

> *Successful learning occurs when learners have ownership of their learning; when they understand the goals they are aiming for; when, crucially, they are motivated and have the skills to achieve success.*

(Assessment Reform Group, 1999)

Many children become aware at a very young age that success is measured through reading, writing and maths and so have often become quickly disenchanted on finding these areas of learning difficult or inaccessible. Many six- and seven-year-old children tell me that they 'can't read', that they 'can't write' and that they are 'rubbish'.

For older students, fear of failing to achieve five A* to C grades may result in disaffection and truancy. It simply cannot be the case that all young people whose test results suggest that they are underachieving are simply less intelligent or able. When we meet learners with an understanding of where they are instead of an expectation of where they 'should be', the outcome is far more likely to be a positive one.

The key priority of an action zone is to raise achievement. This initiative has enabled a deeper analysis of the reasons for underachievement, and has provided opportunities for the development of innovative programmes and projects to address them. Before any significant change in achievement can be realized, learners need to feel valued and motivated. There needs to be a clear understanding of what is to be learned and how it is relevant and meaningful to their lives. The expectations of the teacher must be made explicit and realistically challenging; learners must be given appropriate opportunities to demonstrate and share what they have learned; and time must be allocated for the reflection and review of progress and the celebration of achievement.

If learners have a well-equipped 'toolkit' of skills and have positive dispositions for learning, they are well placed to experience success and a sense of achievement. The Critical Skills Programme is an innovative approach to learning and teaching designed and developed in Antioch in New Hampshire, USA more than 20 years ago, and is now wholly owned in the UK by Network Educational Press. The programme was developed by teachers who were concerned that pupils were not developing the skills and dispositions necessary to be successful in school and in life. These teachers developed an innovative and exciting approach to teaching and learning that drew greatly upon social constructivist theories. Classrooms become effective and safe environments for learning, and learners begin to take responsibility for their own learning through the development of 'critical skills' and 'fundamental dispositions'.

Critical skills	**Fundamental dispositions**
➤ problem solving	➤ lifelong learners
➤ decision making	➤ self-directed
➤ critical thinking	➤ quality worker
➤ creative thinking	➤ ethical character
➤ communication	➤ collaboration
➤ organization	➤ curiosity and wonder
➤ management	➤ community member
➤ leadership	

The Critical Skills Programme has made a significant impact upon teachers and learners. Why is this? The training is experiential, where the participants are actively involved in their learning, so perhaps by being placed in the situation of a learner we revisit the vulnerability of what it feels like to be a learner and recognize that many of the skills and attitudes that we demand of our pupils need to be taught explicitly.

Or perhaps it is that through establishing a collaborative classroom community there is increased value and involvement of every individual and greater recognition of, and therefore greater respect given to, a wider range of skills than simply the academic areas of the curriculum that have for so long been top priority.

Ian Smith, a leading authority in assessment for learning in Scotland, presents key ideas about learning, teaching and professional development (www.learningunlimited.co.uk):

The 7 big messages about learning:

1   intelligence is not fixed

2   effort is as important as ability

3   learning is strongly influenced by emotion

4   we all learn in different ways

5   deep learning is an active process

6   learning is messy

7   we learn from the company we keep

He expands the 'deep learning is an active process' message by stating that 'We learn best when we can make sense of what we are learning. The deeper the level of processing, the more likely we are to retain and make use of our knowledge.'

Assessment for learning is key to the whole process of learning

It is of great importance to engage learners in critical and creative thinking, in the assessment of their own performance and in self- and peer evaluation. Where assessment for learning is central, more of the responsibility for learning is transferred to learners, who may then develop the skills that will enable them to review and evaluate, to make judgements against success criteria and to suggest strategies for improvement.

We know that for deep learning to take place we need a safe environment where we have a real understanding of what we are learning and why, where we have time to think, to review and reflect on ideas, to give and receive feedback, to make our own improvements and to apply our learning in a range of contexts.

In other words, where deep learning takes place, assessment for learning is central to the learning and teaching processes, and learners are motivated, are truly the key 'stakeholders' in their own learning and are, indeed, Successful Learners.

Looking forward

There has been a significant 'shift' in thinking over the past few years, towards recognizing, explicitly, the importance of motivation in raising achievement and building successful people. Recent policy provides evidence of this 'shift'. For the last ten years the emphasis for raising standards has been clearly focused upon teaching. This has undoubtedly been successful in improving the quality of teaching. However, recent Ofsted reports present a clear gap between the quality of teaching and the quality of learning. Happily, the emphasis is now moving from inputs to outcomes as it is learning that is at the heart of the education process.

If our aim is to raise achievement, in its broadest terms, then motivation for learning is critical. As Sir John Lubbock said, 'every child should be given the wish to learn', and the key to this is motivation, which requires the active involvement of the learner. To be actively engaged in the process, learners need to have some degree of autonomy – we know ourselves how much easier it is to engage in a process where our views and ideas are valued. To this end an enabling environment is essential; an environment where all learners experience a balance of support and challenge, where they are encouraged to become risk takers while knowing that it is safe and, indeed, important to make mistakes. It is our responsibility as teachers to provide this environment where learners may flourish – see the diagram below.

raised achievement

high motivation

active involvement

learner autonomy

enabling environment

The improvement of pupil motivation is at the heart of the most recent government initiatives in education. Charles Clarke, in his foreword to the recent DfES publication *Excellence and Enjoyment: A strategy for primary schools*, says

> *Children learn better when they are excited and engaged ... when there is joy in what they are doing, they learn to love learning.*

(DfES, 2003)

The Primary Strategy encourages schools to use the freedoms they already have to suit their pupils and the context in which they work. The goal is for every primary school to combine excellence in teaching with enjoyment of learning.

The principles of learning and teaching as expressed in the *Excellence and Enjoyment* document make very encouraging reading. It seems that many of the issues, which have arisen as a result of a largely content-driven curriculum, have been acknowledged and addressed. It is, however, crucial that real recognition is given to the fact that teachers, generally, are under immense pressure and are working harder than ever. They are required to meet the requirements of the national curriculum programmes of study, to deliver the National Strategies for Literacy and Numeracy, to provide a broad, balanced curriculum, and to ensure that personal, social and emotional needs are met while operating within rigorous health and safety regulations – and at the end of the day demonstrate raised attainment. Sometimes the act of looking at so many individual trees means that we lose sight of the wood. Charles Clarke also reminds us in the foreword to the Primary Strategy that 'enjoyment is the birthright of every child' – so fostering love of learning is fundamental to the process of successful learning.

More recently *Every Child Matters: Change for Children* (DfES, 2004), the government's vision for children's services, focuses upon five key aims to ensure every child has the chance to fulfil their potential by:

Feel safe

Have fun and enjoy my learning!!

Know when and how I have been successful

Know what I could learn next

➤ *Being healthy* – enjoying good physical health and living a healthy lifestyle

➤ *Staying safe* – being protected from harm

➤ *Enjoying and achieving* – getting the most out of life and developing skills for adulthood

➤ *Making a positive contribution* – being involved with the community and society and not engaging in antisocial behaviour

➤ *Achieving economic well-being* – not being disadvantaged from achieving their full potential in life.

The thinking behind this document is far from new, since we know that educational achievement and well-being are inextricably linked. Clearly, this has important and significant implications for all the services that impact upon the lives of children, and success will be dependent upon all the services working coherently together.

Clearly, transforming learning requires great energy and enthusiasm from everyone involved in an organization, but is crucially dependent for success upon the commitment and motivation of the leadership of the school. Transforming learning is also a long-term process, not a quick fix, so time is also of key importance – like any sound investment, you invest significantly early on in order to secure a healthy 'pay out' later on!

> *Adding wings to caterpillars does not create butterflies – it creates awkward and dysfunctional caterpillars. Butterflies are created through transformation.*

> Hebrew proverb

Learn with
other learners

Know why I
am learning

Feel safe

Successful learning: transferring responsibility

Central to the role of the teacher, there needs to be a commitment to empowering learners, a commitment to the transferring of responsibility for the learning from the teacher to the learner and a commitment to making learning meaningful.

Learners need to be enabled to become actively involved in their learning – not simply at the surface level in activity, but by developing understanding at a deeper level. Evidence suggests that there is a strong correlation between understanding and active involvement, which leads to increased motivation and raised achievement. Within an education system that is driven by high-stakes assessment, where attainment still rules, where we are measured by outcome, we must take care not to lose sight of this core purpose. Perhaps the challenge for educational leaders is to move from a 'culture of accountability to a culture of co-responsibility' (McGettrick, 2002) in order to prepare our young people to live well and successfully in the twenty-first century.

The Successful Learner Model is designed to engage teachers and learners in deepening their understanding of the learning process and recognizing how conditions may promote or obstruct effective learning. Observations and reports from teachers indicate that pupils become more engaged in learning as the key elements of the learning process begin to feature in conversations and that pupils are beginning to generate more questions about their learning. With greater understanding of the process, an explicit focus upon improvement rather than correction and the development of skills in self-evaluation, learners are beginning to recognize and enjoy personal learning successes, which increases motivation and leads to greater learner responsibility and raised achievement.

If we strive for excellence, it is vital that learners enjoy their learning experiences and that the environment in which we wish to develop learners is safe and respectful and provides a balance of challenge and support.

There must be planned time for thinking, for questioning and for reflection and review. Learners need frequent and varied opportunities to process their thinking and demonstrate their learning.

Clearly, it is important that there are structures in place to monitor and track learning progress, so that we know how well we are doing – whatever we are doing. We need to be able to identify where progress is good and where it is less than good, so that we can improve. We need reliable data in order to make secure judgements, but it is what we do with the data that is of key importance. If we analyse the information so that we have a clear picture of where learners are, we then need to use this information to ensure that we provide appropriate support, guidance or challenge.

If we take care of all the fundamental principles, we are far more likely to raise achievement than if we concentrate all our energy on simply pushing up attainment levels.

We need all the pieces of the puzzle in place.

It is imperative to combine the acquisition of knowledge and skills with developing positive attitudes to learning, developing a love of learning, so that education becomes person-centred rather than just learner-centred (McGettrick, 2002).

Ferre Laevers of Leuven University was the inspiration behind the development of the emotional well-being and involvement levels, now used in many early years' settings. He describes emotional well-being and involvement as the crucial cornerstones for learning and for life:

> *Emotional well-being:*
>
> *When children feel at ease, act spontaneously, are open to the world and accessible, express inner rest and relaxation, show vitality and self-confidence, are in touch with their feelings and emotions and enjoy life, we know that their mental health is secured.*

Involvement:

When children are concentrated and focused, interested, motivated, fascinated, mentally active, fully experiencing sensations and meanings, enjoying the satisfaction of the exploratory drive and operating at the very limits of their capabilities, we know that deep level learning is taking place.

(Laevers, 2004)

If the well-being and involvement of learners and teachers are kept at the forefront of education, perhaps more learners will experience personal success, will believe that they can be high achievers and, importantly, will have the desire and motivation to do so. More learners will then begin to take real responsibility for their learning and this is the focus for the next stage of this continuing journey of exploration and enquiry.

Have new
and varied
experiences

Have time

Understand
how I learn

Bibliography / Suggested reading

Assessment Reform Group (1999) *Assessment For Learning*, Cambridge: University of Cambridge

Assessment Reform Group (2002) *Testing, Motivation and Learning*, Cambridge: University of Cambridge

Bell, J. (1999) *Doing your Research Project: A Guide for First-time Researchers in Education and Social Science*, 3rd edition, Berkshire: Open University Press

Black, P. and Wiliam, D. (1998) *Inside the Black Box*, London: King's College

Black, P., Harrison, C., Lee, C., Marshall, B. and Wiliam, D. (2002) *Working Inside The Black Box*, London: King's College

Boeree, C. G. (1998) *Abraham Maslow*, www.ship.edu/~cgboeree/maslow.html

Boston University School of Medicine, Erikson Institute and Zero to Three (2001) *The Science of Brain Development* (Brain Wonders), www.zerotothree.org/brainwonders

Brighouse, T. and Woods, D. (1999) *How to Improve your School*, London: Routledge

Caine, R. and Caine, G. (1994) *Making Connections: Teaching and the Human Brain*, Harlow: Addison-Wesley

Call, N. and Featherstone, S. (2003) *The Thinking Child*, Stafford: Network Educational Press

Clarke, S. (2001) *Unlocking Formative Assessment*, London: Hodder and Stoughton

Clarke, S. (2003) *Enriching Feedback in the Primary Classroom*, London: Hodder and Stoughton

Claxton, G. (2002) *Building Learning Power*, Bristol: TLO

Corrie, C. (2003) *Becoming Emotionally Intelligent*, Stafford: Network Educational Press

DfES (2003) *Excellence and Enjoyment: A strategy for primary schools*, London: DfES Publications

DfES (2004) *Every Child Matters: Change for Children*, London: DfES Publications

DfES/QCA (2000) *Curriculum Guidance for the Foundation Stage*, London: DfES/QCA

Dweck, C. S. and Leggett, E. T. (1988) 'A social-cognitive approach to motivation and personality', *Psychological Review*, 95, 356–73

Edwards, A. and Talbot, R. (1994) *The Hard-pressed Researcher: A Research Handbook for the Caring Professions*, New York: Longman

Eggleston, J. (1974) *Contemporary Research in the Sociology of Education*, London: Methuen

Gardner, H. (1983) *Frames of Mind: The Theory of Multiple Intelligences*, New York: Basic

Ghaye, A. and Ghaye, K. (1998) *Teaching and Learning Through Critical Reflective Practice*, London: David Fulton

Giddens, A. (1993) *Sociology*, 2nd edition, Oxford: Polity Press

Gitlin, A. and Smyth, J. (1989) *Teacher Evaluation, Critical Education and Transformative Alternatives*, Lewes: Falmer Press

Goleman, D. (2004) Interview with Daniel Goleman on Emotional Intelligence www.glef.org

Griffith, S. (2003) *Russ finds Old-fashioned Child's Play more than Fun and Games* www.case.edu/pubs/cnews/2003/10-16/russ.htm

Hargreaves, A. (2004) 'Learning, teaching and leading in the knowledge society', papers from UK Workshop Tour 2004 (in partnership with Leannta Education Associates)

Harlen, W. and Deakin Crick, R. (2003) 'Testing, motivation and learning', *Assessment in Education* 10 (2), 169–208. Extracts reproduced with permission

Hitchcock, G. and Hughes, D. (1995) *Research and the Teacher: A Qualitative Introduction to School-based Research*, London: RoutledgeFalmer

Hopkins, D. (2002) *A Teacher's Guide to Classroom Research*, 3rd edition, Maidenhead: OUP

Kolb, D. A. (1984) *Experiential Learning*, Englewood Cliffs, NJ: Prentice Hall

Kyriacou, C. (1986) *Effective Teaching in Schools*, Cheltenham: Stanley Thornes

Laevers, F. (2004) 'Assessment at the level of context, process and outcome: the experiential approach', keynote address at the Association for Achievement and Improvement through Assessment Conference, Brighton

Maslow, A. H. (1943) 'A theory of human motivation', *Psychological Review*, 50, 370–96

McGettrick, B. J. (2002) 'Transforming learning values and citizenship in education', keynote address Graduate School of Education, Bristol University

McIlroy, A. (2004) *We can Build Better Brains* www.globeandmail.com/servlet/story/RTGAM.20040409.wzero10/BNStory/Front/

McNiff, J. (1996) *You and Your Action Research Project*, London: Routledge

McNiff, J. (2000) *Action Research in Organisations*, London: Routledge

Ofsted (2004) *Annual Report*, London: Ofsted

O'Keefe, J. and Nadel, L. (1978) *The Hippocampus as a Cognitive Map*, Oxford: Clarendon Press

On Purpose Associates (1998) *Theories of Learning*
www.funderstanding.com/behaviorism.cfm

Pollard, A. (1990) *Learning in Primary Schools (Education Matters)*, London: Cassell Education

Pollard, A. and Tann, S. (1990) *Reflective Teaching in the Primary School*, London: Cassell Education

Pollard, A. and Triggs, P. (1997) *Reflective Teaching in Secondary Schools*, London: Cassell

Pollard, A., Broadfoot, P., Croll, P., Osborn, M. and Abbott, D. (1994) *Changing English Primary Schools? The Impact of the Education Reform Act at Key Stage 1*, London: Cassell Education

Reed, R. L. (2003) 'Underlying theoretical perspectives on learning', Bristol seminar series, University of the West of England

Reed, R. L. (2004) Paper presented at the Bristol seminar series, University of the West of England

Robinson, K. (2001) *Out of Our Minds – Learning to be Creative*, Oxford: Capstone

Robson, T. (2004) 'Going with the grain of the brain', paper from The Learning Conference: Going with the Grain of the Brain, Success@Excellence in Cities Action Zone, Bristol

Rogers, C. R. and Freiberg, H. J. (1994) *Freedom to Learn*, 3rd edition, Harlow: Prentice Hall (Pearson Education)

Russ, S. (2003) *Why Play Matters* (Playing for Keeps National Conference)
www.playingforkeeps.org/site/why_play_01.html

Smith, I. (2003) *Assessment for Learning: Mark Less to Achieve More* (occasional paper 8), Paisley: Learning Unlimited

Stoll, L., Fink, D. and Earl, L. (2003) *It's About Learning (And It's About Time)*, London: RoutledgeFalmer

Vygotsky, L. S. (1978) *Mind in Society*, Cambridge, MA: Harvard University Press

Zimmerman, M. (1999) *Emotional Literacy Language and Vocabulary: How to Make the World a Better Place Chapter 2*
http://emotionalliteracyeducation.com/emotional-literacy-language-vocabulary.shtml

Index